Follow
that Arrow

Follow that Arrow

that

Notes on Getting Here from There

Gwen Van Velsor

Follow That Arrow: Notes on Getting Here from There
Published by Yellow Arrow Publishing
Baltimore, MD

Library of Congress Control Number: 2016938150

Follow That Arrow: Notes on Getting Here from There
Van Velsor, Gwen, Author
Gwen Van Velsor

ISBN: 978-0-692-66944-0

BIOGRAPHY & AUTOBIOGRAPHY / Personal Memoirs
TRAVEL / Special Interest / Adventure

QUANTITY PURCHASES: Schools, companies, professional groups, clubs, and other organizations may qualify for special terms when ordering quantities of this title. For information, email gwen@gourmetgwen.com

This book is printed in the United States of America.

BALTIMORE, MD

For M.F.B.

one

Every year before Thanksgiving I would watch wild turkeys dive in and out of traffic, roam our front yard, or zip along the hiking trails high up in the jungle. I wanted one on the menu, but in the eight years since moving to Hawaii, had been unsuccessful.

My husband and his hunting friend, a local guy with a penchant for stuffing exotic game birds, would go up to the hunting areas on Mauna Kea every season. They would drive hours into the mountains, well before sunrise, picking their way through lava rock that eats even the finest boots, and trying to follow dogs that were exactly half-trained. These beasts, only allowed out of their pens for hunting, would comb the mountainsides, returning only when shocked by remote electric collars. The men would return at night, a couple of pheasants or a handful of quail in tow, but never the precious turkey.

We'd planned to leave Hawaii that spring, after eight good years in the islands, to live on a sailboat and roam the world like the gypsy travelers we dreamed we were. We had been saving and slaving for many years to make it happen, and I was secure in the idea that everything was finally paying off. I had this fantasy of lounging barefoot on the sunny deck, writing a novel while light winds blew us around the sea. We'd be surrounded by all the time in the world and my creativity would flow freely. The sky would be blue and the water bluer and we'd navigate from island to island, eating like kings from the ocean.

He came home one afternoon in November with two live turkeys in a dog crate. His hunting friend, who worked at a golf course where herds of turkeys diligently destroyed the grass, had trapped them. The golf course did this weekly to try to reduce the population, usually relocating them. This time, they were intended for our Thanksgiving table.

Tired from the hunt, which really just involved shoving the confused birds into the dog crate at the golf course, he decided to wait and kill the birds the next day. Cooped up and panicked, they stamped their feet and scratched at the sides of the crate, turning around and around. We tried to feed them and give them water, but being wild, they wouldn't take it.

On our daily walk, as we watched the dog dive in and out of the tall fountain grass, he questioned my desire to go sailing for the first time, right out of the bluest sky. He told me that deep down, I really didn't want to go. On one side of us lay the ocean, on the other the slopes of Hualalai, our home a flickering light halfway up. The sun was setting and the windows on the mountainside reflected the sparkling orange sun. My dreams hung there in the limbo of twilight.

That night, as I put away the leftovers from dinner, I could hear the turkeys continue to scratch at the kennel. I made him move them to another part of the yard so we wouldn't hear them. He said they reeked. He also said, in nearly the same breath, he wasn't sure about us, in general, together.

Just like that.

He said he needed some time to decide if he should stay or go. I cried into the dishwater as my heart snapped, baffled by the sudden rupture of certainty. I told him if he wasn't sure, then he should go. I didn't mean it. And just like that, without argument, he left.

The next afternoon, he butchered the turkeys as promised. He slit their bodies open, removed their stinking guts, and peeled the skin back, taking all the feathers with it. He was distraught and told me the turkeys were a chore to kill. His eyes steeled over as he described shooting them in the head several times with a pellet gun while they stomped around the dog carrier, not even batting an eye. He had to drive them up the hill and find an open field where he could finish them off with a shotgun. He told me that he would have let them go if they hadn't been so badly injured by the pellet gun. The deed had to be done. He told me all this as he washed the blood from the carcasses off the driveway with a garden hose. He left me with the turkeys, cleaned and ready for Thanksgiving the next week.

I told no one and insisted we pretended nothing were wrong in front of family and friends. He played along. We sat together at the Thanksgiving table, eating the turkey I'd braised in its own juices, savoring the gamey flavor and accepting praise from guests.

Over the following weeks, he came over for long talks, and even spent the night sometimes, but he never touched me, never gave any idea as to what had gone wrong. Sure that he would come back home before the holidays, sure that this was all just a misunderstanding, I sucked it up and powered through, reassuring him that whatever was wrong, we'd fix it together. He said he loved me and cried on my shoulder, but he didn't come home.

Braised Wild Turkey

1 – 2 wild turkeys, feathered, trimmed, cleaned, and quartered
3-4 slices of thick cut bacon
½ cup red wine
1 yellow onion, sliced
2 garlic cloves, quartered
2 sprigs fresh thyme, rosemary, and oregano
Salt & pepper to taste

Wild turkeys can be tough, especially the dark meat, so they need a little extra treatment. Start by cooking the bacon in a deep, cast iron pan over medium high heat until cooked through. Remove the bacon strips and sear the turkey 2-3 minutes on both sides until browned. Don't crowd the pan by putting all the turkey in at once; sear in 2-3 batches. Place seared turkey and bacon strips in a large slow cooker and turn pan down to low. Add wine to the pan and scrape up any browned bits with a wooden spoon. Pour wine and bacon grease into the slow cooker. Add onion, garlic, herbs, salt, and pepper. Cook on low for 6-7 hours, depending on size and thickness of turkey. Meat should fall off the bone when it's ready.

At 4 a.m. on New Year's, smoking sweet cigars with one of those friends you must eventually tell your secrets to, I finally said it out loud. Everyone had gone to bed and the beer cooler was empty, the air still full of firework smoke. My husband had left me, and I didn't know why. I told her I'd do anything to get him to come back home, that I had already done everything. We lit another cigar and blew smoke up toward the stars.

"Well, what's next then?" She asked.

I cringed thinking about the sailboat and all the years of saving and dreaming coming to this unjust end.

"I guess I'm off without him." I replied.

two

I woke up on a Tuesday with tears in my eyes. The sky was just turning from black to gray. The dog peered at me as if to ask if I was seriously getting up this early. But I had to. It was either get up, feed the animals, feed myself, and get dressed, or lie here and slowly die of heartache.

I got up.

Tearing big handfuls of kale and rinsing them under cool water soon became part of a morning ritual. I'm one of those people that wakes up hungry, and as a result, my fridge is never empty. Always slightly obsessive about healthy eating, I honed in on an elimination diet. It was the most extreme thing I could find, and extremes always drew me in. The diet consisted of meat, vegetables, fruit, and nuts. That meant no dairy, grains, beans, sugar, or alcohol. My only salvation was coffee, which I measured out to make exactly two mugs, one in the morning and one in the afternoon.

The pile of greens hissed away in a pan while the same Jackson Browne song looped on repeat. Turning the greens over, I cracked three eggs on top, covered the pan with a glass lid, and then stirred a little coconut oil into the coffee. I forced a comb through my hair and dabbed on makeup, even though it could never seem to cover the circles under my eyes or the permanent creases stretching out on either side. I braced myself for the day ahead.

"And when the morning light comes streaming in, I'll get up and do it again. Amen," Jackson Browne sang from the other room. I sat down at the table, said a prayer of thanksgiving, and smothered the eggs in hot sauce.

I came home one evening to find him playing with the dog on the back porch. A dark pink sunset settled over the ocean below. He wanted to tell me some things. He cried as he told me about the affair, which had dragged on for months now, despite the denial we'd both fought to maintain. The events of the last few months all clicked into place, as did the reaction I'd planned out over many sleepless nights.

I stalked out into the garage and locked the door behind me. As the hammer came down on the headlight of his precious motorcycle, the need for revenge drained from me as if through a funnel. By the time he'd found some keys and ran in to stop me, something had shifted. I'd held a death grip on the idea that if my own husband didn't love me, then no one could. Now, I was no longer able to deny that he was not coming back. As I faced my greatest fear, looking it in the eye and bracing for impact, it morphed into something comforting and kind. Something that I can only describe as God. I knew somewhere in my gut that I was loved, if not by him, then by something greater. I put the hammer down and went to bed.

three

It had become apparent sometime after the holidays that a back-up plan was in order in case my marriage couldn't be worked out. It was not working out. Turning to a list I'd begun as New Year's resolutions, I revised and set that plan in motion. It felt like the only thing left to do.

I began writing to all my friends and family on the mainland, inquiring about couch stays. Plotting a cross-country road trip in the hopes of finding a new home, I scheduled my car to be shipped over. I put in for a leave of absence at work, giving me an entire paid summer to figure out where to land.

Back in college I'd studied abroad in Spain, living for a few months in Salamanca and pretending to study Spanish. Really, it was about weekend trips all over Spain, losing my mind over a boy from Texas, and seeing how long I could go sleeping only during siesta. One of those weekend trips took me to Santiago de Compostela in rainy northwestern Spain. Nose pressed against the train window the entire ride, I was enchanted by the green of the landscape, the little farms, the cobbled roadways, the crumbling old churches. The city itself was full of wonder too: hidden basement bars and windows of unbelievable seafood displays, with platters full of tentacles and shellfish of every color. The evenings were spent listening to church bells and rain in the dark. The days were spent sipping coffee at quirky cafes with mismatched teapots, watching a never-ending stream of pilgrims enter the city.

Dressed in blue plastic ponchos to protect themselves from the rain, the pilgrims filed into the massive cathedral at the center of the city in order to pray over the bones of St. James. They had walked across Spain on the *Camino de Santiago* to get there, following yellow arrows and scalloped shells along the way. There was something mystical and secretive about such a journey that had piqued and held my interest all those years since. Now that my life was up in the air, it seemed like the perfect chance to go back to Spain and become one of those pilgrims myself. Ever since that night in the garage, I'd gotten very curious about God. The pilgrimage seemed like a good opportunity to have some sort of conversation with this being, to actually go looking for this higher power. I began walking at least five miles a day to prepare for the journey.

I cleaned and prepped the house for renting, packing everything away. I even hired a friend to renovate the garage into a little apartment to be sure the mortgage was covered.

At the home improvement store, I picked out a sliding glass door for the new apartment in the garage, finding an employee in an orange apron to help shuffle it onto a cart under the buzzing florescent lights. It weighed at least 400 pounds. I pulled the big Ford truck up in front of the store, and the employee and I could only look at each other and laugh nervously. It was raining lightly.

He had no qualms at all about attempting to lift the door with just the two of us.

"All we can do is try," he shrugged and climbed into the bed of the truck, "it's your door."

As I positioned myself at the base of this glass trap, an older gentleman materialized.

"Whoa, whoa, let me help."

We spent the next 20 minutes twisting, grinding, and strapping the thing precariously into the truck.

The stranger turned to me, almost angry, "Don't you have anyone to help? How you gonna get this out?"

"It's just me," I replied, hopping into the truck, tears pushing at the backs of my eyes. *It was just me.*

As my moving date slowly approached, I felt stronger, faster, and more full of energy than ever. I was in the best shape of my adult life. Packing my things was easy. Saying goodbye to all the friends I'd taken for granted, the friends who cheered me on as I limped across the finish line—that was difficult.

After all my possessions were stowed under the house, I hosted a goodbye party for myself. It poured rain. Water rushed down the street outside as nearly fifty friends, family members, co-workers, and acquaintances piled into the little two-bedroom house. Each person hugged me and wished me the best. Not one of them questioned my decision. They all understood. We shared tacos potluck style and snapped photos in the late afternoon light. A pile of shoes blocked the front door and a herd of little ones circled the tables and chairs.

Every goodbye closed another chapter. I stood against the door jamb with a friend from book club, her husband, and her daughter for a long time that night. Her husband had been burned badly in an accident as a child and words were not his thing. He hugged me, three times in a row. I choked up with the perspective that this situation, this was really not so bad. This man was someone who knew hardship, unfairness, pain. Someone who had done more than survive, who with just his presence assured me that I could do it too. I would be okay.

As the last of my friends packed their kids away in their van, I stood in the kitchen assessing the empty platters and stacked glasses. The dog lapped up the last of the crumbs on the floor, and one of my girlfriends came back inside, hugged me, and began to pray. I sobbed in her arms. It was the first time I'd cried openly.

He came back the day before my plane was set to leave. The rain that had poured every day for the two months he was gone, staying with his folks in Oregon to give me some space, had stopped. It was the finest of Hawaii days, full sunshine and the right kind of breeze. We drove wordlessly together toward the south, past coffee farms and bands of stray chickens, along an oceanside as still as a freshly made bed. The road narrowed and headed straight down a steep cliffside, toward Kealakelua Bay. There were avocado trees and mangoes and streams of guava bushes lining the road. It smelled like coffee roasting and flowers and rotting fruit. Finally, I pulled into the gravel parking lot of the Paleaku Peace Gardens, where we got married those seven years ago.

It was easy to find the place where we'd stood, smiling at each other that day, hearts pounding. Now our hearts were pounding for very different reasons. Hawaii had finally released its grip on me, and I was grateful. We lit a candle and prayed to the God I now knew had been there all along. This man next to me may not have been capable of loving me, but a higher power had somehow lifted me up and out and onward. I couldn't understand how or by whom, but I was loved. As an offering we penned prayers on *ti* leaves before twisting them into cheerful green lei. The sunshine on my face, I fervently thanked the islands, thanked God, thanked the Earth under my feet for this man that had cared for me and cut me open. Our voices rolled down the cliff as we held hands and chanted "*Oli Mahalo*," the Hawaiian song of gratitude.

"'Uhola 'ia ka makaloa lā
Pū'ai i ke aloha ā
Kūka'i 'ia ka loa lā
Pāwehi mai nā lehua.
Mai ka ho'oku'i a ka hālāwai lā
Mahalo e nā akaua,
Mahalo e nā kūpuna lā 'eā
Mahalo me ke aloha lā,
Mahalo me ke aloha lā'"

---

*Translation from Hawaiian: Gratitude chant, composed by Kehau Camara. The makaloa mat has been unfolded, food is shared in love, the great breath is exchanged, the lehua honors and adores, from zenith to horizon, gratitude to God, gratitude to our ancestors, gratitude with love, gratitude with love

I dove into the pool for a final swim on that last day on the islands. Swimming had become part of my regular exercise routine, crucial to maintaining some sort of equilibrium in my life. Touching the bottom and looking up into the bright sun, I savored these moments of peace that being underwater brought. No sound, no talking—just water and sunlight and arms and legs. Lap after lap, I recited silent affirmations with each stroke, "I am strong," *whoosh*, "I am worthy," *whoosh*, "I am loved," *whoosh*, "I am beautiful," *whoosh*, "I am strong."

four

Finding myself on a very different side of the Pacific in Seattle, I picked up my Honda CRV that had been shipped over the week before. It felt sweet and free and new to hop in my rig with my exotic Hawaii plates and cruise around downtown. I spent a couple days in the suburbs with a friend of my sister's, sleeping on a blow-up mattress. Between drinking instant coffee and buying tea and flowers at Pike Place Market, I slowly began to wrap my head around the implications of living out of my car. It was a long way to New York, and I planned to spend a month and a half driving there before flying to Spain to walk the Camino de Santiago.

Heading out to the middle of nowhere on the Washington side of the Columbia River, I stopped for a few days to visit my parents. They live in a log cabin completely off the grid, scrubbing out a harvest each year from a small garden that is enclosed on all sides with double reinforcements to keep the deer and the wailing wind out. My dad is constantly battling to maintain the batteries, well, water pumps, and solar panels. Nothing is ever fully operational. My mom watches from the window, drinking warm white wine and baking bread in a cast-iron skillet.

They love me, they do, and I love them, but it's best for all if I don't stay in the cabin when visiting. The warm white wine has a way of getting between us. Instead I reserved a campsite nearby on the Deschutes River, for the most part away from the wind, if not the snakes.

The ranger at the state park found it very peculiar that I was camping out there alone and checked on me several times each night to see who I've been talking to and to warn me if anyone had been drinking nearby. After a couple days he warmed up and finally asked just what was I doing with Hawaii plates and a car crammed with suitcases and boxes. He gave the usual reaction, first surprised that I was married (I do look very young, a trait from my mother, it must be the oily skin), and then that shadowy look of sorrow common to many when they hear about such a young person getting divorced. He used to be handsome; you could tell by the way he smiled that girls used to find him charming. He warned me a couple times about snakes and fussed over where to park my car to maximize wind blockage for the tent.

A side trip to Portland, where I grew up, was warm and satisfying. You know a place is home when walking down the street feels so old and familiar, comfortable and right. The trees are tall and reaching in Portland, hiding the cloudy skies with their brilliant green. Down on ground level the soft moss could be a bed and the fallen limbs a couch. Clearings are decorated with rhododendron and wild strawberries, and every backyard is a little fairy hideaway. Everyone tends a flower garden, and even the neighbor who never mows his lawn has a dogwood tree or a persistent rose bush that he reluctantly trims each year.

Driving the back roads to the small valley town where my in-laws live, I could smell the strawberry fields as I passed. The green pastures and white farmhouses just about broke my heart in a million pieces. I didn't go to see them, the in-laws, in their big, new house perched in the middle of a wildflower field. Instead I went about my banking business, and then sat down to a cup of coffee and a piece of pie. Raising my mug to the unspoken dream of someday running through those wildflowers, perhaps with a tiny hand in mine, I breathed out a silent goodbye. They were no longer my family; this quaint place with the creek and the open fields was no longer part of my life.

Mom decided to stay with me in the tent one night and we played badminton in the evening. As we patted the birdie over the net without

---

"Wind in the Hair" Tea

This tea reminds me of that breezy evening camping on the Deschutes with mom.

1 oz dried roses
1 oz dried chamomile

Mix tea evenly in a jar. Use two teaspoons of the mix per eight ounce serving. Allow to steep for three minutes in a tea bag or strainer of your choice.

keeping score, she asked me about my marriage—casually—as if she wanted to know what kind of shoes I'd brought with me. As the tall grass poked between my toes, I just shrugged and told the story, recounting the events in sequence—like you do when retelling the plot of a movie. We drank rose chamomile tea by the fire before going to bed early. She slept hard, and in the morning gave me knowing looks. But she never really expressed an emotion. She was after all, just mirroring my own disposition.

The next day, Dad and I met up to go hiking and engage in our mutual habit of drinking too much coffee. He'd taken to slurping McDonald's coffee because it was cheap and they use Seattle's Best, which I'll admit, isn't half bad. We hiked our favorite trail and a spiking kind of sadness hit me when I joked that I would name my first-born girl Wahkeena after one of the waterfalls. He thought it was a good name.

One afternoon, mom made chicken and dumplings for lunch. We bought trays of ripe berries from the farmer's market and hiked in the hills above their town. She used the same old blue and white plates we'd ate on at Grandma's, and set the table in the usual way. She knew that I loved this sort of thing and I genuinely gushed over the spread. Back at camp, I pack up the cooler and say goodbye to the park ranger. His confidence in the way he tells me that I'll be alright, with a wink and a handshake, leaves me hopeful. On a dusty weekday I head east along the river, away from the familiarity of the gorge and onto the open road, blasting music and ugly crying for at least the first hour.

five

Highway 84 is an old thing. It leads nowhere mostly, so it's only the big rigs and me. For several hours all you see is rolling brown hills along the river. Eventually it spreads out, the Blue Mountains in the distance. I arrived in Boise in the late afternoon. My cousins there have two tiny dogs that spin the whole house around. We ate fresh pasta and salad and fish and smiled at each other. We went for a walk around the neighborhood and let the tiny dog lead us around to pee on every blade of grass he passed. Along with a cozy comforter and a hushed goodnight, they gave me my own room in the basement, next to a record collection worth ten times a thousand.

We went to breakfast the next day, stopping at a thrift store to browse the record selection. I bought some teenager jeans that only fit because I was now a ghost of myself following all the stress. Weight had poured off me in the last few months, and it was clear that those who knew me had a hard time restraining themselves from comment. Later, after dinner, we sat on the floor next to the kitchen. In the dark, I told them what was what because they already knew and because they had stories to tell too. It was a relief to let the guard down some. Yes, I was on an adventure, but there were some obvious tender spots that when acknowledged, began to feel less painful. It felt good to hear their stories and their truth—the reality behind the hairdos and the yoga moves and the organic cookies. We sat there a long time and I didn't cry—I just sat there and told my story like I was reciting a grocery list.

I have another set of cousins that live in Boise. Jim, who lived with us when I was small, is almost 15 years older than I, and lives there with his wife and two kids. His wife is one of those folks that other people just don't get, or don't try to get because she is a little offbeat. She was one of the few adults I could actually talk to in my teenage years, so our bond had become the unbreakable sort. They live in a big house in the suburbs with a stone front and plywood floors because they can't agree on what flooring to put in. Their household is like that, an unspoken push-pull.

It was summer, and Tami made kale juice and cappuccinos in the mornings before packing the kids off to baseball or friends' houses. We did things together like get haircuts and stop for iced mochas and eat sweet potato fries for lunch. We went to the horse races and drank red wine and watched nothing on TV. On the weekend, there were baseball games all day and a barbeque after. Jim grilled bear burgers and regular burgers because he's a hunter and because I wanted to eat the bear. Tami said that the bear meat would give you nightmares, and that night I found out that it was true. One starry night, I even slept out on the trampoline in a double sleeping bag with one of the kids.

One night, Tami and I went to an outdoor concert. She made fun of the band, got a little heavy handed with the wine, and more than once gave me the impulse to cover her mouth like a child.

We sat in her big SUV after the show, the windows rolled down to allow the smoke from the clove cigarettes to escape out the windows. I didn't inhale, but I leaned into that cigarette like was the key to my independence. I stared out the window and seriously considered taking up smoking.

"What was he thinking anyway?"

Tami knew I needed this kind of conversation.

"I don't know. He wasn't thinking, you know. He just lost his shit."

We both looked out the window into the empty parking lot. We giggled over the smokes we weren't supposed to smoke as we talked and cried over love and loss. We drove home in the dark on an empty freeway.

The next day we all took a trip to the reservoir in Jim's boat with the dogs and kids and a cooler. It's four-wheel drive terrain on the bumpy roads. The lake was windy but warm, and the kids swam. Jim found a duckling in the bushes and picked it up for his daughter. I found this cruel but unsurprising considering his extensive hunting background. She held it for a time but disliked how it pooped everywhere and let it go. It careened out on the lake, as if running on the water, fast. No one else followed it, but I saw how it disappeared under the water and failed to resurface.

Cousin Jim is like an uncle or a big brother to me. We love each other in a way that's so hard to pin down, something like a mutual admiration. Or maybe we just understand each other. Either way, he is my closest family member and I've leaned on him more than once.

The night before I packed up to keep heading east, Jim came upstairs to check that the fans were working in the hot, attic room where I'd been sleeping on a window seat that had a perfect view of the sunrise. He really wanted to talk, but I could see that words wouldn't help him.

"So what're you doin'?" He asked with the same half smile that I use when I want to ask an important question but don't want the recipient to feel cornered.

"I don't know," I said with as much feeling as my outside self would allow, which isn't much. Somehow a tear escaped and he wiped it away, just like I'd seen him do with his son at a baseball game.

"Don't cry." He pulled me in for a hug and looked me right in the eyes, something I didn't know he was capable of. "I'm sorry about all this," were the words he chose. But that hug spooned my soul. We just stood there like that for a long time, the fans whirring. He wiped my eyes as they ran.

Tami was up early, making muffins for me to take east by mixing carrot pulp and almond flour into a thick batter. I liked Boise a lot. It is near the mountains and lakes, and is small enough to have very little traffic, but big enough for funky coffee houses and good thrift stores. I think coming back here to live is a very good option and I say so. I set off with some kale juice, warm muffins, and an empty tank of gas, barely making it to the station right before the highway on-ramp.

six

I'd driven all the previous day to Utah, stopping only when my eyes were burning so much I could barely keep them open. I asked where to camp at the tourist information center. The woman did not know what a campground was, because she sent me to a motel a mile down the road that let people pitch tents in a patch of grass near the RV hook-ups. Inexplicably, this seemed like a decent idea. I pitched the tent and cooked my dinner in the wind while a group of cowboys who were all together but staying in different rooms stared and stared.

I slept fitfully, and it wasn't until after the sun had just come up on a cold morning that I heard the sound of the rain fly being unzipped. I scooted to the other end of the tent and felt for the pocketknife hidden under my pillow, clutching my cell phone in the other hand. I coughed, just so the weirdo would know I was awake. Footsteps moved away from the tent, over the grass, and back to wherever they'd come from.

After that, I got out of there as fast as possible, finding comfort in Arches National Park just after mid-morning. Among the safety of families on vacation from Missouri and Nebraska and Arizona, I pretended it was totally normal to visit a national park alone on a weekday with your life stuffed in the back of a Honda, snapping photos and buying postcards.

Alone at one of the lookout points, I dug out one of the purple, flower-shaped candles I'd saved from our wedding. Lighting it on a rock overlooking the desert, the candle burned fast and the wax melted all over. I worried for a minute about a ranger finding me there and having a shit-fit over lighting a fire in a national park, but ultimately I let it go. I said a quick serenity prayer and marveled at the white-hot clouds floating over the mesa. My skin burned within an hour out there, so I hit the AC and charged on toward Denver, freedom and glory, with the open desert ahead, behind, and on either side of me.

I rushed through Colorado and South Dakota, stopping briefly to visit friends, admire the Badlands, and have several cups of very weak coffee at a number of spectacularly American diners. My diet consisted mostly of trail mix, pretzels, baby carrots, and caffeine in various forms, save for one dusty afternoon when I picked up a cherry pie after driving through the endless flats of South Dakota. The driving was getting to my head. The running was really getting to my head.

My friend Rose from Hawaii was visiting her mother in a tiny town not far from the Minnesota border, and there was a bed for me that night too. Their family home, set between cornfields and a junkyard, created an immediate nostalgia for grandparents and holidays. I felt an instant affinity for the deep carpet, the matching easy chairs, the permanent pot of coffee, and the pink towels.

After leaving my things on an ancient bed in the basement guestroom, we went for a walk in the last of the afternoon light. The sun was thinking about setting as Rose took me for a tour around the junkyard where she used to play and work as a child. Her family owns the yard and she explained how they sorted the metal from glass from plastic and how money could be made from junking. Nostalgia filled her voice and eyes as we strolled between the heaps of rusted cars and piles of broken glass. Her life had split far, far away from those formative years in rural Midwestern America.

Rose held up a rusted mechanical wheel of some sort, letting it glow in the golden light of the setting sun. She'll never move back here to run a junkyard and live in the old house. She won't eat cutlets and gravy or butter-soaked mashed potatoes at the diner up the road. She'll never again eat fresh, sweet corn right off the stalk because now the corn is all animal feed grade and inedible. But in a world of vegan-paleo-gluten-free pancakes with sugar free syrup, she's glad this place and all its things, junk or otherwise, still exist.

Later on we sat around an oblong wooden table surrounded by shelves of knickknacks. They're mostly treasures scavenged from the junkyard: old blue bottles, a tin Coca Cola sign, little porcelain boxes with missing lids. Rose brought out lots of small bowls with toppings for the vegan tacos she made. Her mother grudgingly ate the meal, expressing that she'd much rather go to the diner up the road next time. I filled my plate at least three times over, overjoyed with this abundance of fresh veggies. It was a comfort and a pleasure to be served the kind of food she knew I made for myself. We talked about the Corn Palace, a glorious castle made entirely of corn, and driving through flat states on my upcoming travels. Rose's smile said everything: she knows what it is to leave and never go back.

Outside the corn swayed in the dark and the highway waited.

Seven

Katie told me right away that she was unhappy. We were sitting at the kitchen table eating lunch and sipping sparkling water. Her giant white dog made circles around the table. Big picture windows faced a large, green backyard with cornfields all around. It was an old white farmhouse that she had, complete with wooden floors and darling kitchen cabinets. They'd moved out here from Hawaii, the unlikeliest of couples. She was the young, Midwestern beauty, and he was the much older local guy with grown children. I'd attended their sunset wedding on the Kona coast. Love had conquered all.

Except corn and Minnesota winters. They were on the verge of a split. We went to a winery in the middle of corn and soy fields, where we walked around a lake and talked and talked about all the things that could be and weren't. Our words formed a tight circle around these big disappointments in the kind of love neither of us believed was real anymore.

At night we all sat around that kitchen table and talked about Hawaii. They shared their stash of island treats: dried mango, *li hing mui* dusted candy, rice crackers. Not one of us wished to be back there. We stayed up late for no reason, making our way through awkward conversation, just to be together and remember what our lives once were.

The next day I walked through the door of Kendra's house in a suburb of Minneapolis with a bottle of pink wine in hand. Ten years ago, back when I lived in Denver, we'd been the best of friends. She'd even come all the way to Hawaii for my wedding and I'd flown out for hers. She looked at me incredulously, baby on hip, as if I'd just materialized out of a black hole. Kendra and I were not always in the best of touch and she hadn't really heard the story of exactly why I was standing in her living room.

We sat on the couch and I told her. Again. Told the story that was now as tired to me as folding towels. She cried. She shook her head. In this little world of backyards and new babies and two car garages, it was not a story that should have been real. Fear materialized, close-up and heavy, as I explained the years that had passed over our marriage. The only thing that held us together was the hope that it would someday get better. The hope that the clouds would pass, and all would be repaired. The clouds passed and left us completely broken. Her eyes grew wider than her baby girl's.

On the Fourth of July we packed the baby in a stroller and walked around a lake.

Her husband had dashed off that morning, despite the holiday, to get some work done at the office. She gave me a look that didn't need explaining. We circled the lake in a haze of if only's and until then's. Around and around.

In the afternoon we went up the road to a little suburban Fourth of July fair. They dressed up the baby and we snapped photos. The sun came out and we giggled at the tweens who'd made matching t-shirts and braided their hair in exactly the same way. We sat in the grass and ate tacos in a bag and I felt one hundred percent American. When the sun went down and the baby with it, Kendra and I drove to the parking lot of the high school.

Fireworks exploded overhead, bright and magnificent. Here we were, little girls in women's bodies, wishing life could always be corn on the cob and friendship bracelets. We turned our faces up and oohed and ahhed with the rest.

Taco in a Bag

I love the Midwest. It is unapologetically American and passing through this part of the country filled me with pride. Taco in a bag is best enjoyed on a hot summer day, maybe after a little league game or in the park with best friends.

1 small bag of Doritos per person
Ground beef
1 packet taco seasoning
Shredded cheese
Shredded iceberg lettuce
Sour cream
Salsa
(any other taco toppings you like)

Brown beef in a pan, drain. Add taco seasoning. Open bag of Doritos and top chips with a little beef, cheese, lettuce, salsa, and sour cream. The perfect picnic fare. Enjoy!

eight

It was Sunday so I pulled into a Methodist church for an early service. Between the old wooden building and needing something to do away from the rained out campsite, it drew me right in. Rain splashed at the stained windows as an old piano pounded out an older hymn. As the pastor approached the podium he tripped on the stairs; the whole place went silent after a loud gasp. I covered my mouth and smiled inwardly.

At the café down the road, big windows faced an empty street flooded with rainwater. A glass case showed off cinnamon rolls and scones and double thick cookies. A group of four guys about my age sat down at the table behind me, talking excitedly about the wind. After noticing I was alone, they offered me a chair at their table.

We all ordered pasties, the regional specialty. They smiled while I explained why I was alone in the Upper Peninsula of Michigan, sipping coffee on a rainy Sunday. They were encouraging and shared stories of their own travels, assuring me that yes, yes this journey was the way to go.

In the span of an hour over breakfast these men shared tribulations over their recent runs for office, their favorite poets, their struggles over having children with severe disabilities, their love for surfing, and their appreciation for this part of the country. It was something about the rain and the coffee that made us share these things. It felt like a time to let some truth leak out.

"So what's the real reason you left Hawaii?" The poet asked me, some stray gray hairs poking out of his messy, dark cut.

And so I told them, coffee mug cupped in two hands, eyes darting from the table to the kitchen and back. They just nodded and all agreed that yes, yes I was indeed on the right path. Yes, yes, I should keep going.

That afternoon the rain cleared some and I hiked along the edge of Lake Michigan. The forest in that part of the country is thick and mossy and full of fairies and magic after a good rain. I collected pockets full of leaves and flowers and bark. Tiny purple buds, rose hips, pale green moss, perfect little white mushrooms. Along the muddy path I found round stones, puzzle piece bark chips, pinecones, and fresh water seashells.

I needed a higher power to help me be rid of the things that were holding me back. Denial. Judgment. Obsession. Fantasy thinking. It was time to let them all go, even the things I was good at. Caring. Smart. Strong. Adventurous. The woman I thought I was, the woman I longed to be. I had to let go of these many versions of myself.

I inscribed these ideas on leaves, and placed them on a piece of bark along with the treasures I found on the hike and another of the purple wedding candles. I lit the candle and pushed the tiny boat off shore, whispering the Alcoholics Anonymous (AA) Seventh Step Prayer:

"My Creator, I am now willing that You should have all of me, good and bad. I pray that You now remove from me every single defect of character which stands in the way of my usefulness to You and my fellows. Grant me strength, as I go out from here, to do Your bidding. Amen."

The wind scattered the leaves over the water and the candle blew out. The sky was gray and dark and unapologetic. I went back to the campsite and fell asleep, waking to a bright day and driving with the windows down along the shore.

Happiness is shared. Sometimes it's shared with strangers in remote villages near the Canadian border. Or with a friendly waitress who doesn't mind refilling the same coffee cup a thousand times. Or with a pasty covered in gravy and a pen on paper next to a big picture window facing a shore lined with tiny cabins. Sometimes happiness comes to us in our loneliest hours, driving across a bridge with white sand beaches on all sides and the sun overhead, illuminating dreams come true.

nine

Leaving my car with a stranger in Albany and hopping on a train with one bag is exactly what free-falling feels like. New York was waiting for me, that beautiful chaos, that perfect mess of humanity just begging you to look in the mirror. For me, New York was three parts obsession and one part curiosity. It was high on the list of possible new homes.

My friend Jessica lived on the Upper East Side in an apartment with wood floors a few blocks from Central Park. While she worked, I wandered the streets and the park, finding peculiar farmers' markets and accidentally buying more groceries than I could carry.

I met up with a with a cousin of my father's whom none of the family had ever met. She lived on Long Island with an ancient cat in a house stuffed with antiques. She believed in the "other side" and got regular visits from those who've passed on. We visited the Walt Whitman house together because he was distantly related to us.

Perusing black-and-white photos and hand-written poems in the museum part of the house, I came across a portrait of Whitman as a young man: having just published *Leaves of Grass*, he posed confidently, hand on hip and hat barely askew as if to say, "*This is me, what?*"

We toured his childhood home and learned more than I'll ever remember about his early life. Out front near a blooming lilac, I posed for a photo in a floor length ocean blue skirt. Hand on hip, one eyebrow raised, I looked into the camera. This is me, what?

Back in Manhattan, Jessica and I put on lipstick and headed to the rooftop of the Met at sunset. I invited my friend Pedro to meet us. We'd met in 105 degree weather on Coney Island a few years prior, during an extended summer visit to the city. While eating a basket of frog legs and fries, we'd connected over a mutual inclination toward anarchist politics and a preference for looking at the world through poetic eyes. That night at the Met he found me admiring a green dress in a temporary exhibit on fashion.

He was short with a nice face and patient eyes. Shy doesn't really describe him. It's more a hesitation or even a slight uncertainty that we should be friends. He refused to get a local beer because it's just too cliché, and instead chose to brood over the outdoor exhibit.

Jessica and I sipped pink champagne cocktails as a golden

sunset rested on the buildings below, stretching out beyond clouds that were exactly the opposite of steel and brick and beams. She is made for this city, my girl Jessica. She's tough and strong and self-assured. She's the woman I depended on to lift me up, to remind me that yes, I *deserve* the life I want. I believed her when she said that yes, I will get it.

After descending to street level and another round of drinks, we walked to the east river. A full moon hung low and tempting right over the water. My enthusiasm for this night in this city was in full force. I get this way occasionally. Sometimes, I do not want the night to end. Luckily in New York, it doesn't have to. I was able to pull Pedro into the vibe but not Jessica. He and I headed for some random jazz club near NYU where we sat on dangerously dirty couches in a basement and bobbed to just the right music.

He eventually leaned in to kiss me and I let him. His teeth scraped my lips and though it was barely perceptible, he was shaking. It was the first time I had kissed someone else in seven years.

ten

Looking up into the tear-streaked face of Jesus, I forgot for a moment that I was surrounded by thousands of tourists. They were taking close-ups of sculptures and buying scads of knickknacks and listening to audio tours in Japanese, German, and Dutch. Harsh, hot sunlight filtered softly though multiple shades of blue stained glass and onto the church floor. We were all there to see Antonio Gaudí's vision, known as the Sagrada Família. Of all the churches I'd seen in the world, this place expressed something raw, unblemished, and honest about the relationship between God and man. Gaudí clearly asserts his love for God, while at the same time managing to mirror the complicated relationship he had with the world as a human being. Ascending the steps toward the altar, I decided in that moment that these were the first steps of my personal *Camino*. My pilgrimage started there, in Barcelona.

I rented a room in an apartment near the city center, mostly to sleep off the jet lag for a few days, but also to enjoy the city before heading out to the French-Spanish border where I would begin walking El Camino de Santiago, known in English as The Way of St. James. The woman who owned the apartment was about my age. Her English was flawless, which is good because I hadn't practiced speaking Spanish in ten years. We sat at her little dining table with a screeching cat at our feet, and she asked me why I'd come all the way to Spain to walk the *Camino*.

I told her about the marriage, the life left behind in Hawaii, and the uncertainty of the future. She told me about the man she was in love with, who she'd recently found out had a wife and a family in New York. We contemplated the elusiveness of love. She remained certain that one day she would find the real thing, which unsettled my stomach.

"He couldn't handle your light; he had to try and cover it, to crush it," she eagerly explained.

I mulled this idea over all the next day, walking the streets of the city. I circled around the Gothic Quarter with a bag of toasted almonds, taking pictures of narrow alleyways, peeling paint, rusted doors, and interesting graffiti. I wandered into Santa Maria del Mar and prayed with eyes fixed on the multi-colored stained glass filling the back of the church. I did a lot of people watching and a lot of wishing someone were with me in the busy square.

There was a bar just across the square from Santa Maria del Pi that had been serving the same hot chocolate and desserts for a hundred years. I met up with an Al-Anon member there and ordered horchata. There was an English-speaking meeting we planned to go to after our drinks. As I related the story of how I ended up sipping a sweet rice drink in this cavernous city, I felt a light bubbling up from deep in my belly. This light pulled me out of this story of heartache and into the headspace of stepping out—stepping forward. Only hours into making the decision that my Camino had started, I was being propelled on, making steps along the open road of change. I couldn't wait to get on the trail and walk it off.

Horchata

Serves 8-10
1 quart rice milk
1 quart almond milk
1/2 – 3/4 cup agave syrup (depending on how sweet you want it)
1 tsp vanilla extract
Several dashes cinnamon

This is nowhere near traditionally prepared horchata, which involves soaking and straining rice or almonds. I love horchata, but I'll tell you right now that you won't catch me painstakingly straining rice in the wee hours. While not authentic, this version is good, and kids love slurping "rice juice."

In a juice pitcher whisk together rice milk, almond milk, agave, and vanilla. Top with cinnamon and keep cold. Top with another dash of cinnamon when serving.

Note: the horchata will separate after a couple hours in the fridge. Just re-whisk and you're good to go.

Navigating the narrow streets back to the subway stop, I marveled at the window displays of chocolate, nuts, and olives. I meandered through an open-air market full of people sipping wine and munching tapas. The streets fill up quickly after 8:00, and being alone, I headed back as soon as it got dark, the light in my belly guiding the way and my feet anticipating the adventure ahead. I thought back to my hostess. My light may have been covered, but it was never crushed. I chomped on a chocolate bar studded with hazelnuts and went right to bed.

eleven

I was the only person left in the train car as we slid into the stop at Irun. The little town on the French-Spanish border is the starting point for the Camino del Norte. I'd chosen to walk this way hoping to avoid the crowds on the famous Camino Francés. The northern route was also known for being the most physically demanding trail. There are many, many routes to Santiago de Compostela, the end point of the pilgrimage. Starting from points all across Europe, pilgrims make their way to the sacred city from north, south, east, and west. Solitude was what I needed to start this little chat with God. But as I exited the station, someone rushed up to me.

"Are you a pilgrim?" He asked in English. "I saw the shell on your backpack." The scallop shell, worn originally by St. James himself, is tied to the pack to mark yourself as a pilgrim.

Together we spotted our first yellow arrow as we exited the train station, pointing the way to the start of our Camino. Yellow arrows mark the trail in its entirety, and are painted on trees, stones, highway on-ramps or any number of places visible to trekkers. Pilgrims depend on the marks to find their way. It was mid-day, siesta time, and the little gray and red-roofed town was deserted. We would start walking the Camino the next morning, but had to wait for the pilgrim's hostel, known as an *albergue*, to open.

Dan was from Hungary and in his early 20's. He'd decided to walk the Camino on a whim and was nervous. He hadn't done much hiking in his life and didn't speak any Spanish. We got something to eat from the grocery store and found a bench to sit on to swap background stories. He wore running shoes and spoke obsessively about how little his pack weighed.

Soon enough another pilgrim joined us, a man about my age with a guitar and a few missing fingers. He had long hair and a very large pack, big black boots and a relaxed smile. He'd been walking a long time already, from Rome, and had a good chuckle at our first day jitters. We were nervous about getting a bed that night, scared that we might lose our way the next day, and fearful of blisters and faulty shoes.

When 4 o'clock finally rolled around and the doors of the *albergue* opened, there was a line of eager pilgrims that filed in. All had brand new backpacks and empty pilgrim passports. Since this was the starting point for most of us, we registered to walk the Camino there. Filling out the application and questionnaire, I sat and thought for a long time over which box to check under "reason for walking the Camino." Finally, I checked "religious." It was God I was seeking, and if he was waiting for me in a church, so be it.

There were several rooms crammed with bunk beds and one bathroom for us all to share. A tiny kitchen housed a stove, a microwave, and an assortment of dishes. The guitarist and I went to the grocery and bought some food to cook for dinner. He laughed at what I selected: chicken thighs, green olives, squash, and onions. This would be the last time I'd cook something like this on the Camino, he assured me.

Chicken and Olives
Serves 4-6

2 TBL olive oil
Salt and pepper
2 lbs. chicken thighs, ideally with skin and bones
1 large yellow onion, chopped
1 cup chicken broth
2 cloves garlic
1 cup pitted green olives (Spanish)

In a large skillet over medium high heat, brown the chicken thighs in the olive oil, sprinkling with salt and pepper as you go, 3-4 minutes on each side. Remove chicken from pan, turn heat down to medium and add onion, sautéing until translucent, 5 minutes or so. Add chicken back to pan along with broth, garlic, and olives. Simmer over medium heat until chicken is cooked through, 15-20 minutes or longer depending on thickness of meat. Share with someone you don't know.

Bumping elbows with French and Spanish and German pilgrims I somehow managed to cook the chicken and make a grand mess. We ate heartily and shared the leftovers. The German convinced me not to pack the extra for my lunch the next day—less weight was better. The Tupperware I'd brought along was the first thing I threw away.

Attempting to read up on the next day's hike in the guide-book, I was distracted by the *hospitaleros*, volunteers who ran the *albergues*, making a fuss over a young German who'd come in with a pack that was already damaged. They were trying to locate a sewing kit to repair the tear. Tobi (I would learn his name over breakfast the next day), was looking a little confused, as he didn't speak any Spanish.

The lights went out at exactly ten o'clock. The snoring had already begun, but I lay there, wide awake, surrounded by young and old from near and far. We were all drawn here to walk, about 500 miles, along the ancient trail. It was bound to be an adventure. I was surrounded by crazy pilgrims who were all prepared to walk until their feet fell apart. Hopefully I'd be left alone while doing the same.

twelve

The terrible fate of instant coffee greeted me the next morning at the communal breakfast. I would soon learn that a real coffee could not be had until well into mid-morning, when cafes and bars opened for the day. Dan the Hungarian rushed off without eating. Nervous about finding a bed that night, he dashed out to get ahead of the others. I wanted to take advantage of the free breakfast and had a choice of cookies, bread, butter, jam, and fruit. Thankful that I'd bought some hazelnuts the day before, I grabbed an apple, cursed my caffeine addiction, and set out alone into the sunrise, away from Irun.

The Camino went straight up into the hills along a dirt track, flanked by houses with barking dogs in their yards. At Nuestra Señora de Guadalupe I stopped to chat with a Pole who'd walked the pilgrimage the year before. He had been saved by Jesus along the way and was eager to fill me in, along with his many tips on how to complete the walk in as little time as possible. He had skinny legs and a large beer belly entombed in a very tight bicycle get-up.

We caught up to Dan while talking about the symbolism behind eating and drinking the body and blood of Christ. I wasn't aware that some Christians believed the bread and wine offered at communion turned into actual flesh and blood. This struck me as equal parts crazy and magical, and I was intrigued. I had taken communion before, but always considered it a symbol of Jesus' death. With this new information, I felt a little leery of attending a Catholic mass, which I'd planned to do along the way. If I didn't believe that the bread and wine were the real thing, was that disrespectful to the church?

We'd been hiking two hours or so at that point and Dan was fading fast. He had been so worried about being the first pilgrim to the next town that he'd burned himself out on the first leg. We had at least a few more hours to go that day so I gave him some of my food and coaxed him along.

We descended down again, along a forested path to the shore. A tiny seaside town with cobbled streets awaited us. Little boats lined an inlet fronted with shops, a plaza, and an old stone church. We stopped into a tiny store and ordered *jamon bocadillos*, the most typical Spanish sandwich, made with shaved ham and bread. The woman behind the counter sliced the meat from an entire cured pork leg. The fat melted into the bread with the heat of the afternoon and made for some welcome walking fuel.

We caught a tiny ferryboat to cross the bridgeless channel

and ascended again, up a thousand vertical steps, right along the shore. The path was mostly dirt or gravel and passed through forest, views of ocean moving us right along. We caught up with Tobi, the German with the backpack debacle the night before, and we all walked in stride together. Solitude eluded me now as I found myself in a tight pack with the Pole, Dan, and now Tobi. We swapped major life milestones the rest of the descent into the town of San Sebastián. It was a hard hike, up and down, and we took turns assuring Dan he would live to see tomorrow.

Arriving in San Sebastian, it was finally time to stop for a coffee. We sat at the outdoor table with our shoes off, proud of a day well-walked. It had been such a lovely, scenic day and we all shared excitement over the days to come. The Pole wanted to continue on another several miles, so we said our goodbyes and meandered toward the beach.

We took our shoes off to bury our feet in hot sand, and the guys went for a swim with the other hoards of tourists. I sat on a towel and finished the rest of my *bocadillo*, telling the guys it was because I hadn't brought a swimsuit. Really, I was irrationally angry at the ocean and didn't want to go near it. Its sparkling sheen reminded me of everything I'd lost half a world away in Hawaii.

We eventually found the *albergue* and went for hamburgers and beers in the pouring rain. That night, Dan offered me earplugs to drown out exactly none of the snoring. But it's easy to get going early when you didn't sleep at all. And by now, I was determined to get up and out before the boys—I wanted some alone time on the trail.

It was no good. They were all waiting for me by the time I strapped my brimming pack on and headed out. A lanky Australian with wavy hair and a tiny pack had joined the crew, and I reluctantly followed along, it being kind of them to wait for me and all. I found it strange that they wanted to walk with me, a woman about ten years older than them, but it was nice to have some company all the same.

Tobi was what every German was meant to be: tall, blonde, good looking, friendly, athletic—the whole package. He was fresh out of school and although his career plans were going well, there was something nagging at him, something he didn't want to tell. He asked me lots and lots of questions that day. I skirted around them as best I could until finally it was out there. I'd left my husband and now I was walking alone in Spain hoping to grasp at a puzzle piece or two in an effort to put my life together.

I cried.

The tears took me by surprise. In all the times I'd recounted my story, emotion had never played into the equation; usually I told it without feeling, robotic. But for some reason, telling it to this boy, hands clutching the straps of my pack, it had finally become real, and I didn't want it to be. I didn't want this to be my story.

"You don't have to tell it," he said warmly.

And so I stopped. The beach town of Zarautz awaited us.

thirteen

The one Euro coin plunked into the vending machine. A paper cup emerged and some gears moved and worked themselves around inside the machine. Finally, hot brown liquid filled the thimble-sized cup. I fitted a plastic lid on top and heaved a sigh, thinking about another morning without real coffee. I headed out the door of the *albergue*, this time getting out before any of the other pilgrims. It was a wet morning, raining off and on. I stood on a cement bench with the deserted beach in front of me, and drank that sweet, instant coffee and munched on some stale bread I'd wrapped up from dinner the night before.

The yellow arrows led me along the shore, around a point, leaving the ocean on my right. As the sun rose, beams of light broke through dark clouds, creating pools of light on the ocean.

The only people around, even when passing through towns, were other pilgrims. I met Pedro from Portugal who was planning to walk around the world. I met two Irishmen, best friends, who managed an incredible pace despite smoking innumerable cigarettes and stopping for beers at every café and bar along the way. We passed sheep farms and cattle herds and hundreds of patches of wild mint. It rained most of the day.

An elevator resting on top of a very steep canyon-like wall took me down into the town of Deba. I sat with one of the Irishman in the plaza while waiting for the train station turned *albergue* to open. It was a newly renovated building, and we practically drooled over the fresh, clean sheets and hot showers.

I walked to the beach at the end of this little canyon-valley town, stopping for picnic fixings along the way. Baguette bread, a greenish stinky sheep cheese, chorizo, a bottle of roasted red peppers soaking in olive oil, a chocolate bar, and some fruit. I sat on a little wooden bench facing the shore and watched the evening crowds. Little kids with surf boards, old ladies dressed in stockings, men with fishing poles and cans of bait. It was warm and I savored the salty cheese and chewy bread.

Later, as I walked back to the *albergue*, a young woman stopped me. Her dark hair was pulled back tightly and she was very thin, wearing baggy pants and a sweatshirt.

"Your boyfriend, he went that way," she said rather abruptly in thickly accented English as we waited for the light to change and cross the street.

"I don't have a boyfriend." I laughed.

We exchanged names and countries of origin and set off together back toward the plaza. By then it was well into the evening, and the Spanish were finally making an appearance. Young and old strolled around the plaza with glasses of wine, ice cream cones, and leashed dogs. We sat and each had a glass of rosé for one euro. We put up our sore feet and talked. Zsuzsanna was a Hungarian living in France and her English was close to perfect. I found myself thinking that it was nice to have another woman around.

Setting out at sunrise was no problem as I'd contracted sleeplessness from all those stress-filled nights back in Hawaii. I used up the last of my emergency Starbucks instant coffee, shaking it up in cold water in a plastic bottle before hitting the trail alone.

The Camino led me up through the forest and to a tiny pueblo, still asleep and wet with morning dew, the rain clouds in the distance giving it a dark glow. Far below, sheep grazed among the blazing greens. All I could hear was their bells and the crunch of my own feet.

Alone at last, my tears came. I let them fall this time. Not for loss or change or hurt, but for the deepest gratitude my small soul has ever felt—how good was God to bring me to this place? To answer the call of my heart? And for a few minutes I forgot what it took to get me here: the lost dreams and the battle cries, the broken hearts and the nerves of steel. I was here, in Spain, walking the cobblestone streets of this tiny town watched over by an ancient old bell tower. Forget long lost dreams, this was very real.

Later that afternoon, I ate the remainder of the picnic fixings from the night before while soaking my feet in a cold stream. I sat on a blanket of thick moss and watched a couple horses graze on the other side of the water. Having finally escaped the boys' club, it was nice to be alone with a good piece of cheese and some much-needed bread.

fourteen

I had stopped to take in another great vista, looking out over stone houses with red ceramic roof tiles. Miles and miles of clouds piled up in the distance. The Irishmen had moved along past me, despite their knee injuries and having managed to get quite drunk by midday. I stopped to snap some photos, and a woman with short, dark hair and a knee brace approached. I greeted her in Spanish and we started to chat. It became clear after a couple of sentences that we both had American accents so we switched to English.

Karin was the first American I'd met on the Camino. We sat on a rocky patch overlooking those infinite, rolling Basque hills, and ate our lunch. We agreed to meet up for dinner or drinks at the next stop, Markina-Xemein.

When I got there, I had to wait for a while for the *albergue* to open. It was hot, the walk had been long and sweaty. I sat at a café and drank an Americano, unabashedly shedding my shoes, a practice rather frowned upon in Spain. When at last we were ushered into the rooms crammed with bunk beds, I spotted my friend Zsuzsanna and bunked next to her. While everyone napped, I grabbed my camera and set about exploring the town.

There were interesting doors and alleyways and fountains in the tiny village. Intricate balconies faced each other along very narrow streets, laundry lines hung between them. The very tops of most buildings sported gargoyles or carved stone borders. Potted plants hung from the street lamps, and statues of important figures stood surrounded by a brick lined square. Two local women, grandmothers for sure, came right up to me with giant smiles. They were dressed in pastel skirts, heels, and soft sweaters.

"Are you a pilgrim?" they asked, arm in arm.

"Oh, yes. I'm from the United States," I replied in my best Spanish.

"Very good, very good." They beamed. "Let us show you where you can take some good pictures."

I followed them through the town square, past historic churches and buildings, through the park, and onto the handball court. The whole time they explained the significance of each site and demanded I take a photo of each one, especially the handball court.

"You speak very good Spanish," they said encouragingly as we said our goodbyes. We all knew that was a white lie, but I accepted the compliment all the same.

That night I shared a meal with Karin, the Irishmen, and

Zsuzsanna. We all planned to head for Gernika the next day, and knowing that there was no *albergue* there, we called ahead to reserve rooms in a pension.

The next day's walk was brutal. It was not only long, but there were few places to stop for a rest. The most difficult part were the several steep descents that wreaked havoc on knees. One of the Irishmen barely made it down—his knees were giving out badly.

I ended up with a room right next to the original boy's club. Liam the Aussie, Tobi the German, and Dan the Hungarian were all there. I was relieved to see them and slipped right back into the posse, with hugs all around. They'd found a monastery to stay in the night before and were now on a very serious search for marijuana. I declined to join them and instead walked up the hill to view a tile reproduction of Picasso's "Guernica," constructed in memory of the bombings that had ravaged the city during the Spanish Civil War.

The next morning around sunrise, I packed up quietly, careful not to wake Karin who'd slept in a single bed across the room. Amazingly, there was a bar (still?) open. The bartender greeted me warmly. She had dyed blonde hair and smudged red lipstick—there was no way she'd slept that night.

I asked for an Americano and sat at the only clean table. Peanut shells coated the floor and beer glasses covered the bar top. Cured legs of pork hung from the ceiling and stung the air with the smell of pig fat. The bartender brought me a little croissant in a plastic wrapper and reassured me that she would add more water to my coffee if I needed it. The truth was that I was dying to have a mug of coffee big enough to fit in two hands instead of the little espresso cups served in Spain. But I just thanked her and said it had plenty of water. Another crooked toothed smile spread across her face as she wished me a "buen Camino" before turning around to finish clearing the glasses from the bar. The comfort of this often-used phrase, shouted to pilgrims by locals wherever they passed, was almost as good as that big mug of coffee I craved.

Walking out into the empty streets, I was greeted by an old man with a cane sitting on a bench. He warned me that I ought to eat a lot more if I were going to survive the journey. I dug out my stash of hazelnuts to prove to him that breakfast was in my future.

I passed lots of farms and gardens of wild herbs that day. I picked handfuls of mint and shoved them in my pockets to make tea for later. I waved to a man in a hat picking peaches in an orchard. He called me over and gave me one of the bright orange beauties. It fit perfectly in my hand. I waited to bite into it until after a steep ascent; it was the sweetest fruit I'd ever tasted.

fifteen

Rain slicked the sidewalks and ran down my poncho as I set out for Bilbao. The Camino took me around roundabouts and through the grubby town of Lezama. A dog with matted white fur and a leather collar approached and I patted his back. He took up stride with me, under over-passes and into a dark forested area. I tried every few hundred feet to shoo him away, but he would not leave my side. I started to think he sensed danger and was protecting me. Finally, in tears, I stopped on a rickety wooden bridge near a horse pasture to wait for some other pilgrims to come along and help.

It was very early so I took off my pack knowing it would be a while for most of the others to catch up. I hadn't slept the night before owing to a late night coffee and a Dutchman. My

Camino was not going the way I'd planned, and I felt disappointed in myself for not being the dutiful, pious, pensive pilgrim I'd hoped to be.

Upon arriving in Lezama the day before, the *hospitalero* immediately popped a bottle of cold, green wine made from an unripe, regional grape. A Spanish couple and a French couple joined in toasting a splendid day of walking. Both couples planned to walk further than I the next day, so this was my first Camino goodbye. Although I'd quickly learned not to bunk near the French (they snored), and the Spanish folks had woken me up more than once before sunrise, I loved them dearly. It was nice to see familiar faces at each stop.

The *hospitalero* worked quickly and efficiently to get everyone drunk by passing around bottles and bottles of the green wine. I escaped this weird scene with the younger group that had arrived, all Dutch. We sat at a picnic table in the sun and drank beers, all of them speaking in English for my benefit. Andres, an older man who'd walked the Camino many times, joined us and told unlikely stories about Camino miracles, laughing and shaking his head every few minutes. He had deep wrinkles, very greasy hair, and chose to walk in fragile-looking sandals. He insisted that he would never sleep in an *albergue*. He packed a bedroll and slept outside every night. We convinced him to at least sleep in the grass outside the *albergue* so he could sneak in for a shower.

Just before the 10 p.m. curfew, the very drunk *hospitalero* insisted that we end the night with a traditional Spanish drink known as *carajillo*. Andres heartily agreed and shoved us out to the bar up the road. A round of espressos with brandy were passed all around. A few sips and it was clear this was undrinkable just before bed. One of the Dutchman, Luc, worried about offending the bartender and *hospitalero*, so he finished the rest of our drinks, probably about five shots of espresso.

On the way back, Luc and I discussed how nice it would be to sleep outside. It turned out that both of us were problem sleepers. He had wavy blond hair and averted his eyes when he spoke to me, embarrassed of his English speaking ability. We made a pact to sleep in the grass that night if rest didn't find us in the dorm room.

A couple hours later, with the snorers in full effect and me still wide-awake, I heard someone jump down from their bunk. Soft footsteps approached.

> ### *Carajillo*
>
>
>
> Don't drink this just before bed like we did. Instead, serve as a brunch cocktail or mid-afternoon warmer on a rainy day.
>
> ½ cup strong, hot coffee (or 1 shot espresso if you can)
> 1 oz decent brandy
> 1 tsp sugar
>
> In a small mug or espresso cup combine coffee and sugar. Stir to dissolve. Add brandy. Sip slowly.

"Are you awake?" he whispered. "I can't sleep."

I got up, grabbed my sleeping bag and followed him outside.

Andres was out there on his bedroll, snoring away. We found a patch of grass and shared the Dutchman's sleeping pad, laying very close. We talked about the stars and poetry and stray dogs and lots of things I can't remember now.

"My heart is going to explode," he whispered. He meant the

caffeine. "Feel it."

I put my hand on his chest and right away felt it beating very fast. His breath warmed my face and I tilted my head up and did the thing I vowed not to do on the Camino: kiss a cute boy. I very much wanted this journey to be about finding God, about rediscovering my independence. Less than a week in, I'd failed at that.

Just then, rain began to fall. Luc found a dry place to sleep under an awning and I went back inside. I crawled back into my bunk, the squeaky ladder nothing compared to the great snoring coming from the French folks. I vowed not to let this slip up become a theme as I stared at the ceiling until morning.

The next day, I set off early to create a buffer between me and the soft-spoken Dutchman. But standing on the bridge with that damn dog, the first pilgrims to come along were Andres, Luc, and his best friend Coen.

Of course.

The dog and I looked at each other, and took up stride with them toward Bilbao.

sixteen

We went round and round about what to do with the dog. Luc and Coen thought I should take him with me to Santiago. Andres was trying to call his veterinarian friend for advice. I wanted to walk back to Lezama and leave him at the *albergue*. Finally, a local approached going the opposite direction and he agreed to take him back the way we'd come. We all decided the dog was most certainly a Camino angel, considering how protective he'd grown of me in only one morning. It turned out that there was an angel with us that day, but it wasn't the dog.

Luc had recently graduated college and was about to enter graduate school in the fall. He wanted to study immigration, and it came across clear and strong that he needed to help others, to find some way to lessen suffering in the world. I listened to him with as little cynicism as I could muster, having held that same mindset in my early 20's. He was eight years younger than myself, and I wasn't sure if I cared. We talked all the way to Bilbao.

It was a short walk so we sat near the river while Coen meditated and I wondered where my maturity had gone. There was a patch of grass under a tree nearby and Luc and I lay next to each other in the shade with our heads on our packs. Randomly, a single violet rose was sitting under this tree. Luc picked it up and gave it to me; we whispered little stories about who'd left the rose and why to each other.

When it was time for the *albergue* to open, we found a locked building with no sign of life. Standing in a plaza, unsure of where to go, a group of excited Spaniards approached us. They said they were from the *albergue* and that we needed to catch a bus to get to the right one. They took us arm in arm to the bus stop, explaining that today was the Feast of St. James and that there would be a big party celebrating pilgrims tonight. We were fairly stunned of our good fortune and obediently did as we were told.

Arriving at the *albergue* was like a family reunion. The Aussie was there, along with Zsuzsunna, Karin, Tobi, and Dan the Hungarian. Hugs were passed all around and we hurried to shower and explore Bilbao. In the old town, we found a place to sit for a glass of wine and tapas. Boisterous conversation erupted as we caught up on all our adventures since meeting last. It felt like I'd known these people for a hundred years.

We headed back to the *albergue* for the pilgrim party, sitting all at one big table. We passed around platters of sausages, cheese, bread, and many bottles of wine. At the end of the night there was a licorice flavored port that was sipped in small glasses.

Flor, one of my Dutch friends, whispered that I ought to hook up with the cute Frenchman at the end of table. He was perfect for me, she pointed out. And he was. About my age, handsome, and walking the Camino for similar reasons. I looked over at Luc, his wavy hair blond hair still wet and shiny from showering. I winced and tried to quash the inner pull that was attracting me to him.

We sat outside in the setting sun on the cement steps and sipped port, discussing plans for the next day. Luc handed me a scrap of paper with a scribbled poem, which I hurriedly shoved in my pocket. It was something about the rose and perfect timing. When everyone went inside he and I walked down the street and sat on the ledge of a rock wall. The stars were coming out and we sat back to back.

"Tell me what you see," he said in his accent that was adorably hard to understand.

"I see stars and a wall." There was a brick building in front of me.

"Stars on the wall. Wow." Lost in translation.

"What do you see?" I asked.

He began to tell me about the man playing with his dog across the street, play by play style. "First the man throws the ball for the dog, then the dog runs! And wait, wait, he gets the ball! Incredible." We laughed and laughed. A certain lightness entered my heart.

The *hospitalero* called to us from the front door; it was time to come inside and go to sleep. We both sighed and dragged ourselves inside. As I crawled into my sleeping bag to the sound of snoring and heavy breathing from the thirty or so pilgrims in the dorm room, I felt the violet rose on my pillow. We were both slipping into something, a certain something I kept reminding myself I did not want. I was here for myself; this was not how my Camino was supposed to go.

seventeen

The Aussie decided to walk with me the next day along an alternate route to the beach town of Pobeña. I was hoping to squeeze past Luc, crossing my fingers that I could get a day ahead of him. The Camino took us above Bilbao, and then quickly into non-descript suburban streets. A Czech with glasses and a heavy build caught up with us, deciding to come with us on the alternate route. There were very few arrows on this route. And then, after half a day of walking, there were none.

We stopped in a gas station. The people there couldn't even show us where we were on a map. My ability to speak Spanish quickly faded in frustration. Liam stayed calm and reassured me every few steps that surely we'd see an arrow around the next bend.

Finally, after having officially lost our way for a couple hours, we stopped in a café to mooch the free Wi-Fi and consult Google maps. The Czech clearly regretted tagging along and ate his *bocadillo* in silence. We figured out that a highway nearby would take us to our destination, just not via the Camino. So we trudged along the side of the road choking down fumes as cars whizzed alarmingly close. Liam tried his best to make jokes and keep it light.

Just when we'd accepted that we'd lost the Camino for the day, a bright yellow arrow appeared on the side of a house. There it was, that blessed path, nestled between two houses and leading off into a cow pasture. Our moods lifted, the sun came out, and jokes were again passed around. The Czech decided to quicken his pace and create some distance; he probably found us most unreliable walking partners. Liam and I waved goodbye and resumed our casual yet deepening conversation.

Liam was in Spain visiting his girlfriend. They'd met in Australia where she'd lived for university. He wanted to do a bit of travelling while she spent time with family and he ended up on the Camino. Just like that. No planning, no soul-searching, no real goal; just something to do. He was hoping that somehow, he and the girlfriend could close the Spain and Australia gap.

"So what's the deal with you and Luc?" He asked with a half-smile. I avoided eye contact. "I saw you guys last night, sitting on the wall. Seemed very close."

"Yeah well you know, he's a lot younger than me and I don't know what I was thinking."

He paused, clearly choosing his words carefully. "But, aren't you married?" We had already established each other's histories.

I took a deep breath and looked ahead to the next arrow. "That's right, I am."

Finally we arrived in Pobeña. There was quite a crowd gathered outside the *albergue* waiting for it to open. The *hospitalero* asked the group for volunteers to sleep on the floor, as there would certainly not be enough beds. Those of us on the younger side of forty readily agreed.

After stashing our bags and changing, we headed to the beach. There was a big group gathered on the sand drinking beers and splashing around in the ocean. I spread out my *pareo* (a sarong for the beach) from Hawaii but still refused to swim. The ocean and I were at war. A constant reminder at each stop of the life I'd left behind; the glitter of the waves had no appeal.

Luc and Coen walked up and joined the group. Of course. I buried my nose in my book and pretended not to notice. Luc sat next to me in the sand anyways and we talked about nothing for the next hour. We exchanged poems scratched on little scraps of paper.

Thinking back to the conversation earlier with Liam, I suddenly felt childish and insincere. This attraction to a man so much younger—it felt escapist and desperate. Did I really like him, or was I just trying to throw a blanket over the pain? I was married. I had nowhere near resolved how that was all going to shake out. I watched the seawater slowly dry on Luc's bare back with a large dose of guilt.

Later at dinner at an outdoor café, my heart was picking up a steady pace as the sun sank down, casting a pink light over the laughter and clinking of dishes. The ocean and I had a score to settle, so this lovely, light potato and vegetable salad would have to wait. I thrust my bag into the hands of a friend and ran down to the sea, knowing our 10 o'clock curfew was coming soon.

The tide was way out and little waves slapped the shore gently and constantly. Walking into the sea was warm, and the water was shallow even 100 yards out. An orange and pink sky chilled the air, and my footsteps were the only ones in the sand. Casting my clothes off as I ran, it was just me and the ocean. I jumped in and let the little waves wash away the surface sadness from my eyes and face and skin. The ocean warmed me and cleansed me and we forgave each other. It was time to begin again.

Renewed and ready to begin walking away from blame, I stepped out of the water toward the boardwalk, the *pareo* wrapped around my shoulders. Luc was there, sitting on the flat rocks. Of course. He'd been watching me.

"You finally swam," he said with a sheepish grin.

"I had to," I answered, shivering. We sat on the rocks and watched the light turn to darkness, talking about serendipity. It turned out Luc had just as many reservations about our connection as I did. Since we kept bumping into each other, we thought it might be the go-ahead from the universe to get to know each other better. We made a plan to walk together the next day.

We walked backed to the *albergue*, knowing we were late and not really caring.

"Come on, come on!" the host said, pointing to his watch as we scurried in to sleep on the floor. He pointed to me. "You speak Spanish, you get a bed."

eighteen

That morning we'd gotten an early enough start to watch the sun scramble out of the ocean. Walking along the cliffside, a calm sea far below, the sun stretched our shadows out long and dark ahead of us. After an hour or so, we decided it was too pretty not to enjoy the view and stopped for coffee. Luc had a little camp stove to boil water and I had more ghastly instant stuff.

So far on the Camino, I'd rarely stopped to take breaks outside of soaking my feet in a creek to reduce the swelling. We walked very slowly that day. I worried a little about being too late to the next *albergue* to find a bed at this pace, from then on known as "Luc style." He liked to stop often. To snap photos, to tell an animated story, to pick herbs on the trailside, to savor another coffee.

Later on, stopping in a little one church town for a coffee in the sun, we smelled bread coming out of a tiny, unmarked bakery. Taking a peek inside, an old woman beckoned to us. We asked for some bread, since that's all there was, and she insisted on giving us the baguette still in the oven. It was piping hot and about a dollar. We shook our heads at our luck.

But then, 'Luc' translates to 'luck' in Dutch, and walking with him made everything feel lucky. He was one of those people that everything just worked out for. All the time. He kept tearing off big chunks of warm bread and passing them to me, and I chewed gratefully. We managed to eat the entire arm-length within an hour. My attempts at maintaining a Paleo diet flew right out the window. I didn't look back.

It was a hot day and after lunch we sat near a stream with our feet in the water, watching little black dragonflies dance among the blackberry bushes. We discussed the names of all the flowers and our wide age difference. Kissing him felt easy and fulfilling, much like eating that warm bread.

By the time we made it to the colorful beach town of Castro Urdiales, I was spent. It was hot and we had a hard time finding the *albergue*. The boy's club was all there: the Aussie, the German, the Hungarian. It was full and our only option was to sleep on the floor. That sounded fine to me since all I cared about was a shower at that point.

A hurried message torn from a notebook lay on my pack when I got out of the shower. It was from Luc. After walking all day together, he'd decided to go on to the next town, leaving me behind with the boy's club. After the day we'd had it was hard to believe he wanted to escape. Maybe these feelings were not mutual after all. I felt a little stupid for getting carried away, but it was probably for the best. I tried to shrug it off and went for dinner with the boys.

The next morning I was up before dawn, checking email on my phone before heading out. There was a note from my husband. When I saw his name in my inbox, emotion overwhelmed me, and I sobbed silently so as not to wake the others. The sky was dark gray and a heaviness descended into my heart. Taking up my pack, I walked along a sleepy shoreline alone. Walking forward was the only thing I had to do that day.

After the wonder of morning ocean vistas wore off, the sun beat me down, and I reached a wall emotionally and physically. I had become infatuated with a twenty-three year-old boy and still had all the unresolved feelings about my looming marriage/non-marriage. I hadn't even really decided if the marriage was over, or if we might try a repair job. I sat at a table in Liendo drinking an Americano very early in the day, and pondered staying overnight where there would surely be no boy's club and certainly no Luc.

Karin the American passed by a short time later. She sat with me and we talked about walls. She'd walked the Camino the year before and just nodded her head that yes, hitting walls was a part of walking this thing. We both decided to stay there and take a half day to relax.

Sitting in the grass, writing in my journal before dinner, Coen entered the plaza. Of course. He flashed a big smile when he recognized me, and having split off from the main pack himself a couple days before, he was surprised to see that Luc wasn't with me. I explained about the note and the bread and the dragonflies. He was more confused than I. He decided to text Luc and see if he wanted to wait for me the next day.

His reply came just as the sky opened up into hard rain showers. Yes.

nineteen

"We are getting a hotel tonight and staying here," Luc announced to the group at a beachside bar where we'd just finished up a round of Cokes. Tobi the German was saddled up to walk another half-day to Guemes and Liam was undecided. The Aussie gave me a look of surprise and amusement. My cheeks were hot.

That morning, Luc had found me walking the streets of an empty beach town in the rain. It had poured all morning, blessing the day with a vibrant rainbow and lightening my heart a little. It felt insane to be chasing after this boy. He'd stayed at a monastery in this town the night before, and even though we'd planned to meet at the ferry crossing later that morning, we'd bumped into each other much earlier, before I could change my mind.

Of course.

We walked barefoot in the wet sand, eating plums and discussing our next move. We'd decided then to only walk another few kilometers to Noja and get a room there to spend some real time together. Feelings were flying and we both aimed to pin them down. It felt like we couldn't escape each other.

Tobi and Liam had caught up to us while we had been sitting on a bench eating soup. The frequent breaks were a theme with Luc. We walked with them along the beach to the bar with the Cokes. When they left, we found a cheap hotel near the church and set about washing clothes in the shower and making a plan for the rest of the day. I went to the beach to swim and he went to gather picnic fixings.

Still without a swimsuit, I went in the water in my undies. No one seemed to mind. Luc brought some warm beers and a perfect little salad he'd assembled back at the room with avocado, cucumber, and tomato. It was heaven to have fresh vegetables. We talked honestly then, about love, about sex, about the great divide of age between us. It turned out we both had some big fears and some bigger doubts about walking this road together, about placing our hands in that of another.

Later that night, we left the room to take a break from each other and this building intensity. We found Liam and some others listening to terrible live music up the road and sat with them for a while. Stopping to sit on the dark beach before heading back to the room, we admired the stars and marveled at how far we'd already walked. Walking all day every day no longer seemed hard; it was simple and satisfying and pure. We sat on some jagged, wet rocks in the dark, keeping each other warm as the ocean breathed cool air our way. As usual, we talked about all things, none of which stuck in memory.

Making love to him was strange and exciting and frightening. I hadn't been with anyone but my husband in over ten years and my body felt like it was made of thin, fragile paper. Luc was gentle, a kind soul with surprisingly confident hands. His arms were a safe place. He was handsome of course, but his goofiness and my age made us an unlikely pair. There was something between us that couldn't be ignored. Something the Camino wouldn't allow us to ignore.

His face changed, darkened, after we finished. The innocent romance was gone. We were all of sudden just two people under a thin white sheet, listening to church bells marking the time in the darkness. Beyond our eyes and ears, little waves slapped at the shore, marking their own time.

The next day, along the way to Guemes, we sat with our backs against the crumbling brick wall of a church. The tall grass was filled with purple and yellow wildflowers. Luc warmed some water to make tea from the lavender and mint we'd picked along the way. I was worried once again about this being silly.

"Can you feel the fire in your heart Gwen?" He asked while stirring the tea, squatting over the flame like a child. "It's something my mother used to say to me when I became worried. I had anxieties when I was young."

"She would say: feel the fire in your heart, the wind in your hair, the earth under your feet, and the water coursing through your veins. Can you feel it?"

I did.

twenty

We arrived at the locked doors of the *albergue* around 5:00 p.m. after walking over 35 kilometers that day, which was much more than a typical walking day for me on the Camino. We sat down, defeated, on the pavement. The Dutchman handed me some bread, which I reluctantly ate.

We'd started that morning at sunrise, a deep pink that lasered out across the fields of misty corn. I drank an Emergen-C in a tiny glass cup and tried not to listen to the conversation the Dutchman was having with the *hospitalero* about a horse trail and "very few arrows." He'd decided the night before to take an alternate route through the mountains to reach El Astillero, a little suburb of Santander. After Bilbao it was mutually understood that we'd try to avoid major cities as much as possible.

I turning my attention to the Aussie, who was eating cookies and milk for breakfast. We agreed to walk with the Dutchman on this alternate route, even though neither of us had much confidence in it. We traded stories for a while of the aches and pains in our legs and backs, and finally packed up to leave.

The morning was dewy and glorious. We picked eucalyptus leaves to shove in our pockets and packs to mask the smell of walking for many days in the same clothes.

Many times that day, we came to forks in the road with no arrows. Each time, using a map and our best judgment, we pressed on, getting lost at least a dozen times, all the while heading in the general direction of El Astillero. We eventually stopped for a long Spanish lunch which included things like braised rabbit, bean and chorizo stew, and red wine mixed with sparkling water.

We walked on and on, stopping sometimes for a coffee or to buy a piece of fruit or to put our feet in a rushing creek. After ten hours (finally!) we reached the *albergue* in El Astillero. Locked. Closed. The Camino no longer passed this way.

A couple of older gentleman talked our ears off about how terrible it was to be stuck here with no place to sleep but never offered to help us. A sign on the door said to call the local police, which we eventually convinced someone to do. Miraculously, about 30 minutes later, a white van pulled up driven by the hospitalera of an *albergue* nearby, in Santa Cruz de Bezana.

She ran her *albergue* out of her home, by donation, and had been called by the local police to come rescue us. This woman's home ended up being the best place I stayed on the whole Camino. Lucky Luc had pulled through again.

An old stone house, with exposed wooden beams, dark

wood stairs and cozy, wool blankets awaited us in Santa Cruz. The house was full of Spanish pilgrims and one crying Pole. For dinner, the hospitalera made us *tortilla de patatas,* a potato and onion frittata/omelet hybrid, which we shared with the other pilgrims around a long table in the kitchen. We lounged on couches in the evening, basking in our good fortune. There was soothing music and good company; it was like coming home.

The next morning, I teared up a little as we left the tiny succulent garden, mewing kittens, and red enamel coffee cups behind. The Camino stretched out before us that day under freeways and over railroad tracks, in the rain and past

Tortilla de Patatas
Serves 6-8

2 russet potatoes, cut into thins rounds (like potato chips)
1 yellow onion, cut into thin rounds
1 clove garlic
2 TBL olive oil
6 eggs
1/4 cup half and half or milk
Salt & pepper to taste

Heat olive oil in a large skillet or non-stick pan over medium heat. Add potatoes, onion, and some salt & pepper and cook until soft, 10-15 minutes.

In a medium bowl, whisk eggs, garlic, milk, and more salt & pepper. Pour over potatoes and onion in the pan.

The next steps are up to you. The traditional way is to cook until the bottom is set (5-8 minutes), slide onto a plate, flip, and cook until set all the way through, maybe another 5 minutes. For those of us who can't be bothered to flip, simply turn down the heat a hair or two, cover the pan and cook until set all the way through, about 10-12 minutes. It is better, taste wise, to flip, but some days it just ain't happenin', right?

dirty little bars into a medieval, walled town.

Luc walked ahead, chatting with some Czechs who looked like hobbits.

"So you and Luc…." The Aussie chuckled.

"So me and Luc."

"What is it do you think? What it is about him?" His walking stick clicked the time on the pavement, those giant boots somehow noiseless.

"He's great, he's kind, he's fun…"

"He's harmless."

"He's harmless," I agreed.

twenty-one

Luc, Liam, and I settled into a private room for the evening. The man at the front desk who had ushered us up the stairs to our room had deep circles under his eyes and no sense of humor. The three twin beds had clean, white sheets and the large bathroom came complete with a cast iron tub. The boys got stoned and played chess in the hallway, surrounded by dark furniture and several oil paintings of Jesus. I soaked in a hot bath, strewn with foraged lavender. My back, feet, and legs had never appreciated hot water as much as they did that day.

Liam and I walked on toward Comillas the next morning, leaving Luc to wait up for Coen. We planned to all meet up for a rest day at the beach. We talked about love being just out of arm's reach, about dreams for the future, about sex. He was the first male friend I'd made in a while, something that seemed more difficult when I was married. We passed cornfields and little streams, a painted red church, and more vistas of the ocean than could be counted.

When after a steep, hot day of walking we made it to Comillas, the *albergue* was full, so the hospitalera helped us find a room in a nearby pension. The owner wore bright red pants and chain-smoked furiously. Red Pants moved us in and out of rooms, squabbling about how much each of us should pay. Rain splashed down as I attempted to hang my laundry on the line, and he almost had a heart attack when I hung it on the porch railing under the awning. He stomped around, cursing pilgrims under his breath, until all that was left to do was laugh. Liam and I found an umbrella and walked to a grocery store for some dinner. We sat on the back porch of the pension for hours while it poured, sharing food and jokes. I felt pretty useful when I showed Liam how to push a wine cork into a bottle when you don't have a corkscrew.

The next morning Red Pants shoved everyone out the door before 8 a.m., claiming that pilgrims do not sleep in. We stumbled down to the beach to wait for our friends. Liam smoked black cigarettes and we took turns jumping in the water all morning. Once again, the conversation turned to love. Once again, I expressed my doubts about Luc: our age difference, my recent split, the timing.

"It seems like there is something very beautiful between you two," Liam remarked, his gaze shaded by sunglasses in the direction of the ocean. Coming from a twenty-one-year-old Aussie surfer, this felt out of place, but warm and affirming. Somehow the lucky Dutchman was breathing life back into a heart that I wasn't sure could feel anything again.

Even though we got to the *albergue* to meet Luc and Coen hours before it opened, there was still a line of pilgrims. Knowing we wouldn't get a bed there and wanting to be alone, Luc and I found a campground on the beach while the others scouted out a more suitable pension.

The campground was full of families with little trailers strewn with twinkling lights, picnic tables full of food, and lots of children roaming around. The beach just below it, a short walk down the cliff, was stunning white sand running against clear waters. It felt like Hawaii. The next morning we rose before dawn, crammed in the tiny one person tent, and jumped in the cold water, naked as babies and happier for it.

We ran into Liam in the late morning and stopped to have a coffee looking out over rolling hills and farms. A family was stooped near the side of the road collecting snails for a feast. We passed by the skeletons of forgotten churches, with trees growing right through the middle. Stopping for lunch on the beach, I noticed black clouds hanging over the river valley that eventually spilled into the ocean. The grubby beach town across the bay would be our stop for the night. As we got closer, it became clear that this was a party town. Garbage coated the streets alongside pools of drying vomit. A sad carnival on the waterfront awaited evening.

"I don't like this place." Luc declared, "I don't want to stay here."

I pleaded with him as we roamed the grocery store. My feet were tired, and it was already well into the afternoon. Didn't he remember El Astillero?

He handed me a chocolate bar with a smile bigger than a watermelon rind. "But I have a good feeling," he said and patted my pack. I followed him out the door and up the hill, away from the stale beach town and right into black clouds.

We walked on opposite sides of the road, silently. I with a chocolate bar and he with potato chips. The road was curvy with no shoulder, leaving us gasping for air each time a car came careening along. We walked and walked, not even passing a house, let alone any other pilgrims who could point the way.

At last we saw a sign for a "*Casa Rural*," which is like a bed and breakfast, and decided to pay extra to stay there. As we headed up the road, he spotted a yellow arrow pointing straight ahead with a capital "A" below it. This was the universal sign for an *albergue*. Not believing our eyes, as we thought we'd long passed the place on the map where the town should be, we asked a man sitting on his porch with an old dog if it could be true.

"Of course." He nodded and pointed up a little side street away from the *casa rural*. From that point on we asked everyone we passed, as this little side street was slowly turning into a town. We were directed into the one existing bar and registered for a bed in the *albergue* up the hill. We were overjoyed at our luck. Lucky Luc was not surprised of course, but very happy all the same; he'd had some kind of intuition.

There was something magical about Serdio, miraculous even, as if the town had come into being just for us. It was an easy thing to believe while on the Camino. From the one bar/restaurant that served the entire town, to the ancient man herding milk cows up the road, to our first taste of *sidra*, a cheap, hard apple cider. The sunset seemed to hang forever over our table where we shared more than a few bottles of the thick, unfiltered beverage and laughed together as if we hadn't just spent the last several hours breathing fire.

"What is your spirit animal?" I asked out of the blue.

Luc had no idea. We looked up his zodiac sign and I told him about my current obsession with Chinese astrology. I explained that my sign, the dog, meant I was loyal and protective.

"And that you follow others," he said bluntly. I climbed into my bunk that night seething once again.

twenty-two

We took off our packs in the hot sun and lay on big boulders by the shore for a rest. Little white sand beaches dotted the coastline and the ocean wore its blue handsomely. Luc's tanned arms rested on his knees and his blond beard framed a carved, angelic face.

A silent, white sailboat came into view. He would have loved this place. My husband would have loved stopping here on the worldwide sailing adventure we'd dreamed of. And here I was with a perfect stranger, broken, lost, and skinny as hell. Fragments of a shattered heart pressed against my chest as I attempted shallow breaths. The pain of each made my eyes well up with tears.

Luc walked on ahead without me to create some space, his

head hanging low. I watched the sailboat drift out of view and then dug one of the purple wedding candles out of my pack. Lighting it near a yellow arrow painted on a rock, I prayed. I prayed for release, for salvation, for relief from the pain of the dream that was ripped away and thrown into the ocean. I prayed as it floated by, just out of reach, between gulping sobs.

I pulled the remainder of a dark chocolate bar out of my pack and gobbled it up before catching up to Luc. We stopped for Cokes served in glasses with large, cylindrical cubes. It was hard to take in the stark beauty of this section of the Camino, and we didn't want to leave it. We decided to camp in Luc's little tent somewhere along the coastline that night.

At a store no larger than a garage, we picked up some pasta, a few apples, a zucchini, and a bottle of sidra. We carefully scouted out a place, right on the edge of a cliff, where we would be fairly safe from getting trampled by cows and out of view of any passing humans.

The sunset lasted hours or years or several lifetimes. Its dark pink glow lit up the nooks and crannies of the craggy mountains behind us. The serene, rolling waves below us crashed against the cliffs with gentle force. The ground cover was spiky with little purple and white flowers. We gawked and gawked at the beauty of Cantabria, bringing our pasta to a boil and sharing the sidra. As the stars came out, a thin chill settled in. It permeated my bones, my sleeping bag, my hands, and the inside of my throat. We made love that night under the moon, but I was not there at all.

The next morning we decided to walk alone and meet up later—I'm no good to anyone pre-caffeine, plus I was sure Luc was looking for an out after the sailboat breakdown. Both of us continued to second-guess this relationship for different reasons, and we both had doubts about walking together that morning. The Camino ascended and descended sharply, above horseshoe shaped beaches and tightly clustered red roofs. An excitable Spaniard began giving me lectures on how to properly wear my pack and then demanded we have breakfast together in the next town. In Llanes we found ourselves navigating through hordes of tourists. When the Spaniard looked away, I gave him the slip.

I caught up to Luc mid-morning in a little touristy beach town. Llanes was without question full, and every other place we'd passed was either too expensive or full as well. We grabbed some food and weighed our options, noticing some campground signs in the area. At the very busy and crowded campground right on the beach, we were able to rent a camper trailer for next to nothing. It felt like a little home, complete with beds, a kitchen, and curtains for the rusted windows. Coen met up with us later and pitched a tent on our site. He commented that we were like a married couple, with a house and everything, which made my skin shrink and crawl.

I went down to the beach to enjoy a lunch of cured sausage, bread, a hunk of stinky cheese, and an apple. The boys hung back to catch up on adventures since they'd been apart. We swam and sunbathed all afternoon. I made love to a large bottle of Coca Cola and read Shadow of the Wind on my Kindle. My throbbing feet were grateful to the feel of sand and cool water without the imposition of shoes.

That night we went for dinner at a real place with forks and knives and wine glasses. We were served whole shrimp that had been grilled on a piece of wood along with salad and bread and an ethereal sidra-flavored cake. The boys taught me lots of Dutch words I can't remember, and we laughed into the warm night.

The crowded campground finally went to sleep after midnight, and those little curtains eventually lulled me to sleep in the hot trailer. Luc placed a hand on my side, solidifying the relationship we had found ourselves in. I shied away, trying to get a slice of my own on the little bed. It was not time to be someone's other half. Luc was especially good and sweet and kind. All of the things that I was not.

Shrimp a la Plancha
Serves 4

2 lbs whole shrimp (head on if you can find it)
2 cloves garlic, smashed
1 lemon
¼ cup olive oil
Salt to taste

Leaving the shrimp whole, wash and devein, removing shell on center of shrimp if desired, as in leave the head and tail on. In a small saucepan, heat the garlic in the olive oil on medium low until fragrant, 3-4 minutes. Discard smashed garlic, add juice from the lemon and some salt, set aside. Heat a BBQ grill, cast iron grill pan, or regular cast iron pan over high heat. Grill shrimp for about 1 minute on each side, or until opaque. Place shrimp on a serving dish and drizzle with lemony oil, adding more salt if desired. Serve with crusty bread and a fresh salad.

twenty-three

I sat alone in the kitchen, my head reeling from an intense hangover. I sipped a little of the drip coffee I'd so longed for, dipping crispy ginger cookies into the hot liquid. My hands were shaking and my eyes felt crusty and dry and puffy from crying. I heard footsteps on the stairs and quickly wiped my tears. It was Luc.

"I'm ready to go now," he said, his pack already stuffed and clipped for the day. Without question I jumped up, washed my coffee mug and found my shoes. He waited for me at the bottom of the stairs, pointing the way to the back of the house where the German couple that ran this tiny *albergue* had built a tiny meditation cottage. We sat on red pillows in front of a nativity scene and closed our eyes. I prayed, hard, for forgiveness—for one more precious day with this incredible soul next to me that, by now I knew, I'd completely taken for granted.

We'd come across this house with bunk beds upstairs and comfy lawn chairs outside the day before. We were welcomed with open arms and even fed dinner. We sat around their large table with a rowdy bunch of Spanish men, mostly about my age. Luc was definitely the outsider with his limited Spanish and handful of years that separated us. We passed salad and home-made pizza, wine and bread. Our hosts encouraged us to walk into town that night for the local *fiestas*— something of a town-wide party. I was very aware of being the only woman in the group.

We set off just as it began to get dark, taking a short walk down dusty streets lined with old stone walls to the down plaza. Our Spaniards emerged from the local bar, each with two bottles of *sidra* in hand. We saddled up to a picnic table and they began pouring glass after glass, chugging with abandon. It is tradition to pour the cider from up high in order to aerate the sour stuff. According to them it was also tradition to chug it as fast as pos-sible. *Sidra* splashed all over our feet and hands and clothes.

The guys began begging me to dance, to speak in English, and to chug cider with them. It was easy to get caught up in the dancing and selfie snapping and singing weird Spanish drinking songs. Luc joined in but quickly became the butt of their jokes without him really understanding. Soon, he got sick of being the odd man out and wanted to walk back to the house. I wanted to stay and enjoy this break from our typical early-to-bed pilgrim evenings. Luc agreed to stay a little longer, wandering away from the group to listen to a band play on the other side of the square.

We played carnival games and the guys gifted little junk bracelets and trinkets. One of them walked with me into the bar to use the bathroom. On our way back to the group he pulled me close and kissed me. I let him. I turned around to spot Luc watching all of this. He shoved his hands in his pockets and stalked back toward the house. I let him. I was certainly no one's girlfriend.

The next couple of hours were a blur as we continued to drink and play carnival games and exchange email addresses. When the guys started taking shots of hard stuff and wanting to dance roughly, I wanted to go home. None of them would walk with me so I set out alone, around 2 a.m., into the night.

At the very first crossroads it was apparent I didn't know how to get back. There are no streetlights in rural Spain. I attempted several different routes, but got more and more lost. I was sure a dog was going to jump out and eat me at any moment. I stood in the moonlight and cried before heading back toward the *fiestas* to ask for help. The guys were standing in the same spot, drinking the same shots, and cheered when I appeared. I tearfully asked them to walk me home until one of them finally gave in.

My feet covered in sticky *sidra* and coated in dust from the roads, I crawled into Luc's bunk. He turned over, held me, and didn't say a word.

The next morning when he wanted to walk together, I followed. This was supposed to be our last day before he continued on with Coen and I split off onto the notoriously challenging Camino Primitivo. Neither of us wanted our time together to end like this.

As we walked into the sunrise, cornfields surrounding us on

all sides, Luc stopped. I looked into his face and began to sob. He pulled me close, and we stood like that in the middle of the street for a long, long time.

"Why did you do it?" He finally asked.

I couldn't speak.

I was angry. Actually, I was full of black, sooty rage. And even though I'd taken it out on Luc, I was angry with myself. For screwing up my marriage; for walking the Camino with a man instead of alone; for allowing Josh to lie to me again and again and again. I wanted someone else to feel that pain, and the only person to direct it towards, out there in the middle of Spain, was Luc. And now I'd done that; I'd hurt him, caused him pain he didn't deserve.

We walked together mostly in silence, stopping for lunch and a nap on the beach. Now that our time was coming to an end, we wished for time to stop and rest for a couple days here on the coast. But Coen was waiting for Luc and the Primitivo was waiting for me. My body was weak, dehydrated, deflated. My soul was wounded and sorry and guilty. Luc sliced up some hard-boiled eggs, some cheese, bread, and fruit. He passed me a cold Coke and a makeshift sandwich, offering more when I had eaten it all.

"You have so much pain. I'm sorry for that," he said confidently, brushing hair away from my face. Of course I followed Luc. Of course.

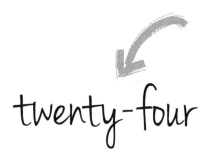

twenty-four

Just after departing from the Camino del Norte onto the Camino Primitivo, I saw a hawk on a low-slung telephone wire. He looked me right in the eye. This route, known for being the most physically challenging, is what I came to Spain for. On this route, I was sure, my feet would meet their match. Bring it on. These next weeks were what I'd prepared and trained for, and the challenge I'd intended for body and mind.

On a bridge looking out over the tall mountains promising hard hikes ahead, I chanted *"E Ho Mai,"* the Hawaiian request to enter.

> *"E ho mai i ka ʻike mai luna mai e*
> *O na mea huna noʻeau o na mele e*
> *E ho mai, e ho mai, e ho mai e**"

---

* E ho Mai by Edith Kanakaʻole. Chant is repeated three times. English translation: Grant us knowledge from above, The things of knowledge hidden in the chants, Grant us these things

This time my intention was clear: allow me to pass through this place and allow me to find the way. I prayed that finally I would get some solitude; that finally I would commune with God, who seemed far away from my heart at that moment. I was ashamed of being distracted by Luc, on this once in a lifetime chance to connect with God and with myself.

The night before was damp and rainy. Luc and I had found a cheap room in a pension and said our goodbyes with hands and mouths and breath. When I wrapped the dirty white sheet tightly around my chest the next morning, I had to stop myself from asking him to come along on the Primitivo. Something about the morning light, his hair wet from the shower, and the freckled skin on his arms felt like a beautiful alternate reality. A reality that existed more fully that I'd experienced before. He looked so beautiful to me, the kind of beauty that has no other source than a higher power. It occurred to me then that maybe I had been alone this whole time. Maybe Luc wasn't real at all. Maybe he was a guardian angel, a psychotic episode, or the illusion that had finally sent me into insanity.

I dressed quickly and rushed a goodbye, stopping for coffee in hopes that caffeine would bring me back to the real world. At the way marker indicating the split from the Camino del Norte, I left a note for Luc, along with a pile of mint leaves. I'd scribbled "thank you" on a piece of waxed paper and secured it on the cement marker with a stone. Then I turned left, toward the mountains and into the forest.

I did not see any other pilgrims all day nor any other coffee shop. I was one of the first to arrive at the abandoned monastery that now housed an *albergue*. The walls were painted with dripping blood and phrases in Spanish about the importance of stopping in Oviedo on the way to Santiago. The Camino Primitivo is called as such because it is one of the oldest known routes, dating back to medieval times.

Since most pilgrims were now a few weeks deep into their Camino, "families" were well established. Since I'd left my Camino family behind on the Norte, I was feeling a little left out and lonesome.

A big Camino family came prancing into the monastery, quickly taking over the kitchen and shared eating area. I joined them, eating my first Paleo meal in weeks, a can of peas, a tomato, and a package of sardines. While the women mostly ignored my presence, the men enthusiastically encouraged me to walk with them the next day to Oviedo. I declined, both because I wanted to be alone and because Oviedo was more than I cared to walk in one day, about 38 kilometers.

Thus far I had somehow managed to escape any physical injuries. No blisters, no pulled muscles. I attributed this to limiting the distance walked per day to 30 km, the training and preparation I did before arriving in Spain, and the frequent rests. In fact, I was in the best physical condition of my adult life, and this journey was mine for the taking.

I sat in the cloister outside with a man from California. He was Catholic and attended mass every day while on the Camino. I didn't know that there was a mass every day, or anything about Catholicism except for what I had learned from the Pole who told me about Communion on the very first day of walking. I asked him if he thought I could take Communion at a Catholic church. He said yes, as long as you believe in that moment when the bread touches your tongue that it is the body of Christ. As in, the actual flesh of Jesus Christ. I didn't know if I could go there.

Averting my eyes when one of the Spaniards from the drunken *sidra* night arrived, I winced at the memory and hoped he wouldn't notice me. Three more of them walked in a short time later and tried to chat me up. I retreated to my bunk, embarrassed and afraid of what they might tell other pilgrims. So much for my fresh start.

twenty-five

Fog rolled over the countryside below the rock wall where I stood snapping photos. An old man drove a herd of cattle up the cobblestone street and a couple of the guys from the Camino family I'd integrated with the night before were nearly in stride with me. Max, from the Netherlands, had walked all the way from his front door, his eye on Santiago. He had a long beard and a nice smile and was overjoyed at the few Dutch words I could speak. He was in somewhat rough condition after walking many, many weeks through Europe. I recognized him immediately as someone just as lost as I was.

The rest of the walk that day was slow, rainy, and mostly along roads. I didn't want to admit it, but I was feeling sick. This forced me to stop in the next town versus continuing on to Oviedo with the Camino family. I tried to convince Max to stay, but he didn't want to break the bond with his family. I shopped for some food and had an Americano while waiting for the *albergue* to open. Sardines, a tomato, and fruit was for lunch. Bread was off the table again as I tried to get back into a Paleo groove.

I was the first to inhabit a bunk and quickly unpacked to lay down for a rest. My throat was sore and my body ached so I fell asleep quickly. A loud group of voices roused me not long after. Incredibly, it turned out to be a group of the dreaded Spaniards, whom I was sure would have been at least a day ahead of me by now. They were joined by two other men and were very interested in making sure we all went out for *sidra* later. We all chatted politely. Since there was no chance of a nap, I settled for a soak in the very new and clean showers. So far, I was the only woman and it was a real luxury to have a hot shower alone.

As I was finishing up, a voice at the door said, "Can I come in?" It was one of the new Spaniards speaking in broken English.

"Uh. What? Ok." I said, without really thinking. He walked up to the shower stall.

"Let me in." His voice was rough.

"No. What do you want?" I made sure the stall door was locked.

"Open the door."

"No. Go away." I couldn't tell if this was a joke but it was certain the others could hear this exchange down the hall. Expecting that one of them would intervene at any moment, I stood there calmly waiting it out.

"Open the door! Open the door!" He started to shout in

Spanish and pounded on the stall door.

"Go away!" I yelled. There is no way the others couldn't hear me. He kept pounding on the door. I started to panic as it was clear no one was coming to help me. His shoes paced back and forth in front of the stall and I began to wonder if there was enough space for him to crawl underneath the door.

"Leave me alone!" I screamed in Spanish. He grunted and began to retreat. I searched for something sharp in my toiletry bag, and prepared to stab with nail clippers and tweezers. Finally, his steps left the room.

I turned the water off and sat on the tile, adrenaline flooding my head and heart and veins. I could still hear voices down the hall, so I waited until it was quiet. After a good amount of time, when I was sure he had gone, I came out to find someone had thrown my clothes from the bunk onto the ground. I looked at the Spanish guys I knew from the *sidra* night, not believing that they didn't help me. They kept their heads down.

That night I evaded them by walking to the town square and hiding out with some hot tea and the Internet, my head pounding. I choked down a horrible dinner of greens and eggs made in a dirty microwave and drank cup after cup of lavender tea. I feared this was punishment for what I'd done to Luc and that I'd never escape these men. That night I tossed and started with every sound, afraid for my safety, knowing none of these men would protect me. The gang returned drunk late that night and dropped quickly into their bunks, thankfully.

I was up and out before daylight, desperately trying to escape. Praying with all my might, I wished that I could have another chance to express my regret to Luc for needing the attention of those men that night. I was exhausted, terrified, alone, and kicked myself for not staying with the Camino family from the day before.

Although the walk was dreary, the city of Oviedo was stunning. The sore throat and headache that had plagued me the night before seemed to have been walked off by mid-morning. After stashing my things at the *albergue*, I walked around and around the city, marveling at the architecture. Inside the cathedral I felt the presence of thousands of pilgrims that had come before me, and cried at the feet of tombstones of those who'd lost their lives attempting to reach Santiago. People had died on this journey, doing what I was doing, and my heart could barely take the gratitude I felt for walking where these people had walked. I stared for a long time at a piece of bloody cloth behind glass, once used to mop up the wounds of Jesus, and looked into the tearful eyes of a wooden Mary.

Outside the sun was setting, casting a pink glow on the plaza. I snapped some photos and floated around, stopping in my tracks when across the street the Spanish crew approached. They were too close for me to turn around or duck out. They waved enthusiastically, big grins on all their faces. I cringed inwardly and with my entire face.

Taking up the rear of the group was Luc, smiling as always. Of course.

twenty-six

He ran across the street without looking for cars. His cheeks were flushed and his hair and breath smelled of *sidra*. The Spaniards walked on, away from Oviedo, as Luc pulled me in for a hug around my neck.

"What are you doing here?" I was less stunned than completely enchanted. Only Luc could appear out of nowhere on the streets of Spain.

We sat on some steps nearby and just laughed, both agreeing this was some kind of miracle. Luc had seen my scrawled note on the way marker and decided at the last minute to take the Primitivo. As he took the left fork, saying goodbye to Coen, he knew I would be at least a day ahead of him. If I hadn't been sick, we never would have crossed paths.

Luc suggested we go to the cathedral to thank God for bringing us together, overwhelmed by the generosity of the Camino. Sitting in the front pew, I whispered to him the prayers I'd tearfully spoken to God just hours earlier. We got on our knees.

Later that afternoon, I found myself being scorned and berated by the *hospitalero* for asking if Luc could sleep in my bunk that night since the *albergue* was full. But he eventually said yes, and we crammed our packs in the tiny bunk. The building housed about fifty pilgrims and was filthy from top to bottom.

We retreated to an alfresco restaurant to celebrate our reunion with a glass of wine and some fine Spanish cheese. The evening wore on while we excitedly reviewed the guidebook; we were in this Primitivo challenge together now. Children played in the plaza in the last of the evening light as their parents passed around tapas and half glasses of beer. I squeezed Luc's hand.

"I want to walk together."

"Let's walk together Gwen."

Getting a late start the next morning, we quickly began to scale a very steep slope above the city. The path was lined on either side with blackberries, which we stopped to pick and eat. Luc laid on the grass for a quick nap—we hadn't exactly slept well crammed in the bunk the night before.

A few kilometers later we stopped again. Luc was looking pale and felt weak, refusing the bread and fruit we'd brought with us. After consulting the guidebook and another pilgrim walking by with two dogs, we discovered that the next town had a small *albergue* we could stop in if needed. Less than an hour later we arrived in this town, nothing more than a bar and a butcher shop with one shelf of bread and produce. Without much argument from Luc about stopping here, we got the key to *albergue* from the bar.

He fell asleep immediately. Thankfully it was very early in the day and no pilgrims had arrived yet, so he could rest in quiet. I set about making soup in the filthy kitchen. The *albergue* had no toilet paper, soap, or cleaning supplies, but I cleaned up the garbage and swept the floor before catching a nap on a bench. When I woke up, an Italian couple sat on the bench beside me, heads bent over a guidebook. The woman, a pretty thing with curly hair and naturally red lips, had walked the Camino before, and this year was bringing her boyfriend along. He was much older than her, but spoke good English. He made it clear that he was very unexcited about the lack of food options in this town.

I went inside to check on the soup and Luc only to find a lesbian couple with shaved heads pouring it into bowls so they could use the pot. I rolled my eyes and asked them to wait while I washed some Tupperware. Luc was still fast asleep. A Spanish man and his elderly father inquired if he were all right. They gave me some strange black pills to soothe his stomach and clucked their tongues in concern.

Despite the dingy conditions, the view from the *albergue* was incredible. Craggy mountains pitched sharply under dark clouds, thousands of shades of blacks and greens and grey. As a child, views like this, when the other side of the mountains couldn't be seen, fascinated me. I would wish so hard to be able to look just beyond the visible, as if something mysterious waited on the other side. Maybe it was true.

Luc woke just as the sun went to bed, still feeling sick. He ate some soup and drank mint lavender tea with me and swallowed the black pills. He worried some that he wouldn't be able to walk much at all the next day, but I assured him we would walk together, even if it meant stopping for a few days.

He shook his head. "I'm really grateful that you are taking care of me."

"Of course, Luc." I rubbed his back.

That night as a sweet Polish family sat in the stairwell singing, a van arrived with a troop of musicians. They unloaded their instruments and began to play some kind of Celtic folk music. While Luc slept in his bunk, I watched from the big, glass windows as the other pilgrims filtered downstairs.

The leader of the troop led the group in a dance, all in one circle, changing partners as they stepped round and round. They laughed as the leader corrected their wrong turns. Luc came up behind me, his face still a little pale.

"We should dance," he said. He pulled me away from the window and into the parking lot. We learned the steps side by side with the lesbian couple, the Poles, the Spanish man, and his father. We laughed at our mistakes and held our sides with the effort of jumping and twisting. Stars twinkled over this tiny mountain town and eventually the musicians packed up and slept in their van.

All that walking had led somewhere; apparently I'd made it to the other side of those mountains. Mystery and magic was exactly what waited here. Stepping beyond the window glass needed some nudging, but I was doing it; I was joining world instead of observing it.

twenty-seven

I had been on the Camino for nearly three weeks. Every day was different and every day was the same. Wake up, drink ghastly coffee, walk, find a bed, take a shower, wash clothes, eat, try to sleep. The vortex of the Camino allows pilgrims to shed their everyday worries, leaving their hearts and minds more available for other pursuits. I regretted the days when I allowed others to make me feel rushed, hurrying to the next stop only to find plenty of beds and wishing I stopped to admire the view longer, savor a Coke, or chat with more people. There were always pilgrims who insisted on waking before dawn to ensure a bed at the next stop. And yes, there had been times when we'd missed out on a bed, but there was always another option around the corner. Walking with Luc calmed me, helped me to relax into just walking, and got me to trust that rushing would get me nowhere.

We made our way to a crumbling, abandoned monastery just on the other side of the river from a one-grocery town. Luc was feeling better, but we still took it slow. The *albergue* inside the monastery had nice facilities for pilgrims, so we joined the Polish family, the Italian couple, the Spanish father-son duo, the lesbians, and the musicians in the communal bunk area. It was a festive reunion and already we were forming a Camino family on the Primitivo.

After dinner Luc and I sat with our feet up on a park bench facing the old monastery. The Catholic Church and Communion and Jesus were on my mind again. I asked Luc what he thought, if it were okay for a non-Catholic to go to mass and take Communion. Raised Catholic, he seemed to think it was all right, even if I couldn't stomach that the bread and wine were the actual body and blood. I considered this strange idea, again, not wanting to trample on the ideals of the Church.

"What if, just in that moment, when you eat the bread, you believed it was the body?" Luc suggested. "You don't have to believe it now, or after, or ever again."

As we walked back to the monastery, a thin shawl wrapped tightly over my shoulders, the doors of the chapel opened. Old ladies with coiffed hair and pastel sweaters filed in. Luc gently shoved us toward the door as the bells rang for evening mass.

We sat in the middle of the sanctuary, half understanding the Spanish mass. I looked over at him for cues on when to kneel, cross my heart, or bow my head. The time came for Communion, and Luc looked at me with eyebrows raised. I got in line with the others and looked up at the stained glass above, surrounded by stone that was surely about to come crashing down with age and neglect. Placing my hands the way Luc showed me, I took the bread. I chose to believe, in that moment, that this was real. Kneeling down to face the altar, Jesus looked down on me from the cross. The wafer stuck to the top of my mouth and I knew without question, in a warm, bottom of the gut way, that this piece of bread was indeed His flesh. I knew, as the many pilgrims who have gone before me must have known, and the many pilgrims after will know. I tucked this knowing deep inside myself, wrapped tightly in the fellowship of those who also believed. Luc put his arm around me as we walked back; I wouldn't have gone in without him.

The next day's walk was a long one. I wanted to start early to avoid the heat. Luc wanted to sleep in, so we agreed to meet at the *albergue* in Tineo later that day. A little over half of my brain thought we'd somehow get separated.

"Trust me, I'll be there," was Luc's answer to my anxiety. That word, that request, made my fists ball up and my skin go numb. I felt scales creep over my heart in protection.

I was out into the foggy darkness even before the Italians. They waved goodbye while sipping their *cafés con leche*. The trail was steep and rocky, making for slow walking. I stopped in the next town to grab some things for lunch and my first coffee of the day. The woman at the café served it with a banana, wishing me a *buen* Camino. I sat inside and savored the moment of peace.

In the next town I stopped for twenty minutes at least to see if Luc would catch up. It was slow going for me, so it seemed like he could have been behind me at any moment. Another mile down the path I stopped for a coffee at a dirty little place, this time waiting for an hour. No Luc. The Way took me higher into the hills above the houses and farms. I stopped to sit on a flat rock overlooking the steep trail ahead, put my head on my knees, and fell asleep. My heart was heavy and I could barely breathe. Surely Luc should have caught up to me by now.

Feeling dizzy, sick to my stomach, and abandoned, the only thing to do was to get up and keep walking. Soon the path became very muddy and wooded, with no light allowed through the dense trees. I approached a couple, the woman in a long skirt, sandals, and a thick sweater. The man had a long, dark beard and carried a very heavy, polished staff. They were from France, her English barely intelligible; I liked them immediately. Philippe had walked all the way from France, his girlfriend joining him somewhere halfway. They never slept in *albergue*s, only under church awnings or at rough campsites. His girlfriend was cheerful but hesitant to share his enthusiasm for the journey.

Philippe and I talked a long time about pilgrimages and the beauty of taking each day one step at a time. Constantly moving forward, into what, we never knew. He described the trust he had to gain in life by walking the Camino. He had relaxed weeks ago into not knowing where he would sleep, what he would eat, or how difficult the walk would be. He asked me how I was doing with it all, and I was honest. I needed to be: that day on the Camino, I was having a difficult time trusting that it would work out for the best. I was sure Luc had stayed back, letting me get ahead.

"You will be okay," he said, very confidently. I knew he was right.

When the French couple stopped for a break, I pressed on. I could see that a steep descent waited just ahead. My knees were calling to me that day and the brick path didn't help. I rounded the curve to find the *albergue* in Tineo behind a chain link fence. I waved to some of the Camino family who'd made it in hours before, and out of the front entrance walked Luc. Of course.

He ran up to me, very worried. It was late in the afternoon, as I had taken about ten hours to walk 25 kilometers.

"You're here," I said and began to cry. "How did you get in front of me?" Another mysterious miracle of the Camino.

"I've been waiting here for hours. I thought you wouldn't come." Relief poured out of us, released from the tight grip of mistrust.

We skipped the *albergue* that night and got a private room in a pension. We only left the room to eat later that night, clutching onto each other in gratitude, exhausted. It had felt like a test. I felt uncertain if I'd passed.

twenty-eight

The next few days were known for being the toughest climbs of any of the Camino routes. Known as *Hospitales*, the day-long trek ascended through nothing but ruined, medieval pilgrim hospitals, where many who had come to walk the Way had perished due to harsh conditions. The quiet chatter among pilgrims on the trail, gathered around dinner tables, huddled in front of sinks, and hand washing their socks, had reached a fever pitch. Luc and I found ourselves at an *albergue* on the side of the road among a few houses surrounded by farmland. The owner included meals with the price of the rooms, and as we passed around platters of empanadas, roasted pork loin, and stewed vegetables, the conversations became increasingly fervent. Some pilgrims were even considering an alternate route to avoid the climb. I was feeling strong and ready to take it on.

The next day, I left Luc sleeping and began the ascent on a cold morning. Pretty purple alpine flowers appeared among the wind-blown shrubbery the higher I went. Views of endless farmland and vertical cliffs accompanied me, though I only stopped to snap a couple photos and to eat the lunch of pasta with tuna and olives that Luc had made for us the night before. I took off my pack, my hat, and my shoes, and sang "*Oli Mahalo,*" the Hawaiian song of gratitude, as the cows looked on. My legs, calves, and back went unstrained as every cell, fiber, and wavelength of my body and mind moved through this moment I was born for. Every step was joy, every breath was full of the knowledge that I was in the exact right moment at the exact right time. On this most difficult day of walking, I felt free. A great start to a new life.

Bright sunlight fell on my back as I made the descent into a town that turned out to be only a few stone houses, a church, and a bar. Luc caught up with me there; we had a coffee and exchanged stories about the hardest day of hiking yet, a day which had felt easy for me. Luc had gotten lost somehow and had a run-in with a pervy old man, so he hadn't had the same "fire in the heart" experience I'd had.

The *albergue* in the little town was filling up fast, so I reserved a space. Luc was feeling jittery and unsettled, and wanted to keep walking. So he went ahead and we agreed on a place to meet up the next day.

The closer we got to Santiago, the dirtier the *albergue*s became as more and more pilgrims joined the trail. This one was no exception: cold water showers, bunks with no sheets, a very dirty kitchen, and nowhere to sit and relax. All that I could do was retreat outside and lay in the sun.

Joined quickly by a rowdy and diverse Camino family, the afternoon turned into a series of guitar serenades on the lawn and a lengthy, but successful search for four-leaf clovers. I joined the new crew for dinner in the dirty kitchen: a twenty-something German, a Spanish doctoral student, a middle-aged American blonde who only talked about sex, and a boisterous Dutchman who was too tanned for words. The evening wore on and we discovered the travelling musicians were playing down the road for a big crowd. Under the cold, clear stars, I was finding that I very much missed making random friends on the Camino, something that had become increasingly rare with Luc in tow.

The next day I sang with Italians, crossed over a huge dam, just about wore my knees out on a slippery descent, and met up with Luc at a restaurant looking out over the dam. The red-lipped Italian and her boyfriend were there, along with the French couple that I'd come to adore. It was good to see some familiar faces.

Not so for Luc. He had a rough night, ending up in a town with no facilities and in an *albergue* with only non-English speakers. We finished the day's tough climb and grabbed a room in a pension, right next to the French couple who had finally given up sleeping in church doorways for one night.

We treated ourselves to a luxurious Spanish four-course lunch and a long siesta. We strolled around the plaza, picking mint for tea, and talking about our childhoods. We ultimately wound up at a café for coffees and free Wi-Fi. I had a message waiting for me from Liam, who had hung back for almost two weeks to go to a music festival with his girlfriend on the coast. He was online and wanted to know where Luc and I were so we could meet and up and finish the Camino. An hour later a lanky figure with a head of messy hair walked by the café. Liam. I dashed outside and grabbed him by the arm, hardly believing it. He had hopped on a bus just a little while earlier and landed right here, which put some perspective on how far we had actually walked.

We enjoyed a happy reunion, sitting just beyond the plaza in the dark, boiling mint tea and passing around snacks and stories. Grape vines swayed in the breeze on either side of us. Liam described how he could have gone back to Madrid with his girlfriend but felt compelled to finish the Camino. It was nice to be back in the fold of this family.

Over the next couple days, Liam saddled up with us, giving me a welcome break from coupledom. The guys walked ahead of me always, leaving juice boxes or granola bars on the trail, or writing my name in stones. Liam cared for my foot when I got my first pulled muscle, and we found ourselves sleeping in a gymnasium on cardboard boxes, next to the French couple, when the *albergue* was full.

One afternoon on the long, hot way to Lugo, we sat in some grass on the roadside sharing bread and soup. Luc stirred the soup over his camp stove as Liam entertained us with surfing stories. A quiet wind rustled up the rows of corn in the fields nearby.

"Have you ever considered that only one of us real?" Liam asked.

In fact, I had.

He continued. "As in, I'm real, but you and Luc are figments of my imagination because I've gone crazy on the Camino." I'd considered the possibility that Luc wasn't real many times. I'd also considered the possibility that I'd gone crazy.

"So which of us is real then?" Luc asked.

We all looked at each other intently and laughed. They mostly agreed that I was the best candidate for being a living human being, but in the end it was left up in the air.

We sat there for a while dipping bread in the soup, wondering who was craziest. I wondered if any of this were real at all and took a bite of an apple.

twenty-nine

The octopus was served in large chunks, steaming in a thick broth, with tentacles as big as dimes. We sopped up the liquid with stale bread and French fries, toasting a job well done on finding this hole in the wall. We were taking a rest day in Lugo, notable for its city center that was surrounded by a medieval wall wide enough for strolling on the top. Tourists in strappy sandals lingered at cafes on the inside, old ladies pushing carts of groceries circled the outer ring. This tavern we'd found was on the outside of the wall with only three tiny tables and a wooden bar. Our bellies were overjoyed.

The octopus was followed by a soup made from greens and potatoes called *caldo*, then barbequed pork, salad, and cheese-cake. We finished the night with an espresso and a silent pass by the old cathedral, the center of every Spanish city. I'd even commemorated Lugo by buying some new clothes and running a comb through my hair. We allowed ourselves to forget about being pilgrims for a couple days and settled into being tourists.

We sat on a park bench eating bread and maple syrup. I'd found a bottle at the grocery store after discovering that Luc had never heard of it. We toured the church and said a heartbreaking goodbye to the French couple; our rest day would leave us far behind them. We had a picnic in the central plaza, laughing and people watching and letting our toes breathe. It was good to just be: no walking, no planning, just settling into the idea that this other world was about to end.

Luc had gifted me a yellow charm bracelet earlier in the day. It stood out against my deeply-browned skin and reminded me that only a few days separated us between here and Santiago. Only a few days separated us between here and goodbye and the inevitable return to the real world.

We walked down to the river for a coffee and some sightseeing in the late morning. Liam had gone off on his own, and it was just us again—together virtually every moment of the day. Maybe it was the hot sun or tired feet, but I pretty well laid into Luc about not being able to meet other people because we were always together. We decided it was best to walk on our own for a few days after leaving Lugo, planning to meet up again in Santiago. I felt relieved for the space.

The next morning we set out early, planning to go our own ways after lunch. This day was the last on the Primitivo, as it would soon join with the popular Camino Francés and all the throngs of pilgrims headed to the same place. I was bracing myself for an end to having quiet paths all to myself, but a couple hours into the misty morning Luc's foot began to seize up, causing him to limp. We rested, contemplated, and finally decided to stop at the next *albergue*. He had hoped to catch up with Liam, but that wasn't going to happen. We were together for another night. It was becoming clear that some outside force was keeping us together and in stride as we walked the final stretch of the Camino. Despite the occasional exasperation at feeling a little suffocated, having him with me was comforting. We were so close to the end, and I in no way felt like my life path was clear. I still felt bitter guilt for allowing my marriage to fall apart. I still had no idea where I would go from here.

We found a large patch of blackberry bushes along a creek near the *albergue*. It was sunny and we lay in the grass before finding a *casa rural* to grab a non-alcoholic beer and a sandwich. The cats in residence caressed the legs of our chairs as we shared a simple meal of fresh, country bread, fluffy omelets, and soft, salty Galician cheese. The evening sunlight warmed our faces, and we stretched the moment out by sitting silently, smiling at each other.

We scrambled over a windy mountaintop late the next morning, Luc's foot taped and temporarily fixed. The day was cloudy and stark, and the jagged boulders said something fierce. On the other side of the mountain a little cabin appeared, a couple with a child standing on the porch drinking coffee. They beckoned us inside to view their little gallery and to sip tea. We were surprised to find Liam inside chatting with one of the artists. A brief reunion ensued and the boys walked back to meditate on those jagged boulders in the wind while I walked ahead on my own.

Soon I came to a crossroads. There was no one around. It was just me and the Camino, surrounded by purple and yellow alpine flowers and skinny pine trees. Ahead of me the road stretched on, clearly marked with a bright yellow arrow and a cement way marker declaring how many steps were left to reach Santiago. On the left, a gravel road ascended a steep hill topped with a few motionless windmills. On the right, a path lead into the forest, seductive and dark. Behind me were the many, many miles of Camino worn by my own feet as well as those of all the pilgrims that had come before, and all of those that would come after.

It occurred to me then that I didn't have to follow the yellow arrows at all, that a more interesting path could surely be found by hanging a right or by blazing my own trail through the trees. Eventually I'd get there. The only way to ensure failure would be by going back the way I'd come.

At that crossroads, my life became clear, distilled in a way I finally understood. There were always arrows pointing the way—we could choose to follow them, or not. More than likely we'd end up at the same place anyhow, but it's up to us whether to take the clearly marked, far easier road, or to go off the rails and down our own path.

After considering the options for a moment, I followed that arrow.

thirty

The *bocadillo de tortilla francesa* had quickly become my staple meal, as making the effort to stumble through narrow grocery stores with a heavy pack had become extremely unappealing. For only a couple bucks, I was served an entire baguette stuffed with a plain omelet. Something about the simplicity and sheer size of this sandwich was deeply satisfying to my soul. Now that the Primitivo had merged with the Francés, there were not only herds of pilgrims, but also far more and far cheaper food options. It was easy to let self-catering go.

That evening I snagged the last bed in an old stone *albergue* by a sweet little creek and a matching stone bridge—Luc and Liam had decided to press on to meet up with Coen in the next town. The *albergue* was buzzing with excitement as most pilgrims planned to walk the al-most 40 kilometers into Santiago the next day. I had other plans. The guidebook described a giant *albergue* with 400 beds just four kilometers from Santiago. I liked the idea of walking into the city at dawn.

By mid-morning the next day, I had already come across the gang waiting for me with cof-fees in hand. Luc was in bad shape. The muscles on the top of his foot were tight to the touch and he could barely limp along. After lunch in the shade, the guys went off ahead while I hung back, keeping pace with Luc. We stopped every hour, for sodas, a soak in a cold creek, or to make our last batch of mint lavender tea. Lots and lots of pilgrims passed us, until at last we seemed the only pilgrims left on the trail.

Bocadillo de Tortilla Francesa (French Omelet Sandwich)
Serves 1

1 baguette
2 eggs
1 TBL butter or olive oil
Salt & pepper to taste

In a skillet over medium heat, melt the butter or oil. Whisk the eggs in a separate bowl and pour in with butter or oil, allowing eggs to set on the bottom, 1-2 minutes. Use a spatula to flip the eggs into an omelet. Allow the eggs to fully set, about another 2 minutes. Cut the baguette in half lengthwise and stuff with omelet. Toast the bread first if you prefer.

"Can you feel the fire in your heart Gwen? The wind in your hair? The Earth under your feet? The water coursing through your veins?" Luc said again as we toasted the Camino with our tea.

I just laughed. I felt all those things. As much as I'd resisted him, it was this goofy angel that had been patiently guiding me along. Running a hand through his blonde beard on this last day of walking, knowing that the end of something strange and magical was approaching, I felt grateful for loving Luc. My guilt had passed away. I wanted to remember him just like this, big black boots, sweaty t-shirt, blue eyes crinkled in a permanent smile. For as much as I'd pushed him away, it was Luc who showed me how to slow down, how to enjoy every step, and how to live again.

At last we approached the turn off to the final *albergue* where I would stay the night. Liam and Coen were already there, shirts off and drinking beers. They'd been waiting for us all afternoon. They shared the good news that some of our friends from the original crew back in Bilbao were in Santiago, having already walked the loop to Finisterre and back. It would be our last chance to reunite with everyone. I felt pangs of guilt for wanting to stay back. But this was not a time to follow the crowd, no matter how much I wanted to see my friends.

Luc visibly sucked in his second wind, taking his shirt off for the final push into Santiago. I watched the three of them walk down the street before finding a bunk amongst the 400 others. I had a little lavender left in my pocket and brewed some tea as the sun went down, vowing it would be my last meal before taking Communion in the cathedral at pilgrim mass the next day. I have no idea where this need to fast came from, only that something compelled me to do it.

Before any trace of light the next morning, I stood on the pedestal of a Camino statue with a view of Santiago below. As glimmers of daybreak appeared, I chanted the request to enter, the request for knowledge, as I had done many times in Hawaii.

"E ho mai i ka 'ike mai luna mai e
O na mea huna no'eau o na mele e
E ho mai, e ho mai, e ho mai"

A light rain danced as my final footsteps took me into the city, as group after group of pilgrims stopped to don their plastic blue parkas. Just as I remembered from college, I walked into old town Santiago, toward the cathedral—just one of millions of pilgrims who had come before, who joined the throngs now, who would arrive after. The spires of the cathedral shot into the gray sky as I approached the plaza, smiling and warm and alone, but for the pulsing collective.

Pilgrimage complete.

Physically, I was relieved and ready to stop walking. Mentally, I was confused. Where was my clarity?

While in line to get my official hand-signed *compostela*, Luc and Liam walked out of the main office. We passed congratulations around before Luc and I set off for the mass in the cathedral, leaving Liam to secure our rooms for the night.

The pews were completely packed, and Luc had to sit on the floor. The priests and monks and nuns filed in. We waited our turn for the body of Christ, and once again I felt an inexplicable realness when eating that bit of bread. Once again something electric happened in that moment. I allowed myself to believe the bread was flesh. I didn't know what to do with the feeling or what to say, but I kept it close to my heart and out of reach.

Wanting to celebrate our walk with a big dinner, we settled for burgers and *tartas de Santiago* still warm from a bakery. We made circles around the plaza, waving to all the pilgrims we'd befriended or even just recognized. Back at the pension, we sat around eating potato chips, drinking red wine, and talking about going back to the real world. Most of the gang was set to leave within the next two days. I had almost two more weeks before my flight departed Spain and no plan for how to spend the time. Instead, I found myself thinking about going to the beach or to Portugal or even to Holland with Luc.

Luc, Liam, and I went out for drinks at several of the underground bars around the city. It was just the same quirky place I'd remembered it to be in my college years: hand-muddled drinks, vintage music posters, cavernous basement nooks only open after 2 a.m. At our last stop the whole crowd got into singing and dancing to Elvis while passing shots of vodka around. I slipped out and up the stairs, and found myself at the foot of the cathedral. Lit up with spotlights and swirling with fog, the ominous moss-covered stones shut out the sounds of revelers and deafening music. The silhouettes of the spirits and saints carved in the stone looked down on me imploringly. It was clear to me that this journey was nowhere near over.

thirty-one

It was rainy in Santiago. Pilgrims hustled by at all hours, tucked in their parkas, walking sticks clicking along on the cobblestones. The coffee shops were crowded with folks on their way to work and tourists escaping the weather. I was headed back to the cathedral for an English speaking mass, a leaden heart dragging me all the way. The service was held in one of the side chapels, its uneven wooden pews filled by all walks of life.

A woman with short gray hair and a red sweatshirt helped the priest lead the service. We were asked to go around and introduce ourselves before the body of Christ was offered to our lips. I prayed fervently for direction. After the service, the woman with gray hair offered to sit and have coffee, should anyone have the time. I followed her and one other woman up the street for an Americano and a slice of *tarta*.

We started with small talk, watching the drizzle. When the other woman excused herself to go, we began deeper conversations about our reasons for being here. She had a slight mustache and an Irish accent and a soft way of speaking and smiling. I didn't hesitate to admit that my marriage had failed and that I had come to find my way, or something like that, and that direction seemed very far out of reach. She was here to volunteer with the church and help pilgrims.

"Do you have children?" She asked me. When I shook my head no, in a sorrowful way that came straight from my guts, she replied, "That's a relief." It was and it wasn't. Tears seized my eyes.

"Do you have any children?" I asked.

"Well my dear, I'm a nun. So…no," she said without judgment of my naïveté, but with a fair amount of amusement. I covered a laugh, acknowledging I knew nothing about the Catholic faith. Something lifted then and we talked honestly about God and Jesus and those big tears rolling down Mary's face in the chapel. I asked her about divorce and shared my fears of sliding in the wrong direction.

"I promise you," she said softly, "if you ask, He will reply. God is speaking to us all the time, we are the ones that need to open our ears to hear." It seemed so simple, yet I'd never asked God to speak to me. She offered some numbers to call should I be interested in using my extra time to volunteer in an *albergue*.

I spent the next two days with Luc, saying goodbye to friends as they departed Santiago on buses and trains and planes back to Australia and Holland and France. We enjoyed fabulous food and coffees and a nice hotel room and talked about everything all over again. The impossibility of a future together loomed obviously and heavily over our heads, but we still talked circles around it, wondering if we really were meant to be together post-Camino.

I was drawn back to the cathedral again and again and again. Finally came the morning of the next English speaking mass. I had an appointment later that day to arrange for a volunteer position at an *albergue* in the city, thinking that's what God was leading me to do, pay it forward to other pilgrims. I sat in the pew looking up at Mary, her lacy collar tight at her throat, her face serene despite the pain.

The reading for the day came from Luke 9:23-24: "And He was saying to them all, 'If anyone wishes to come after Me, he must deny himself, and take up his cross daily and follow Me. For whoever wishes to save his life will lose it, but whoever loses his life for My sake, he is the one who will save it.'" The words surrounded me in a very deep, gentle knowing. I knew God was speaking directly to me: "take up the cross and follow me."

With this new knowledge in my heart, I called the *albergue* where I was going to volunteer to get directions. It was a wrong number. I tried again. "Take up the cross and follow me." I knew exactly what it meant, but I had exactly no desire to keep walking. I looked down at the new clothes I bought myself and around at the cozy hotel room. It was the last night together with Luc. He was leaving for Holland by bus and it was back to tennis shoes and a sleeping bag for me.

I hopped in the giant bathtub, sure it would be my last chance to bathe in hot water for the foreseeable future. Luc came back to the room from saying goodbyes to the last of our friends.

"Did you get the job at the *albergue*?"

"No. I'm walking to Finisterre."

"Earth Under the Feet" Tea
Makes one pot

Luc and I would pick fresh mint and lavender almost every day while walking, saving it to boil later for tea.

4 sprigs fresh mint (or 1TBL dried)
4 sprigs fresh lavender (or 1 tsp. dried)

Bring six cups of water to boil. Using a strainer or large tea bag, add herbs and allow to steep for at least three minutes. Since this in an herbal tea, you can allow it to steep for much longer if preferred, as it will not turn bitter.

thirty-two

Finisterre lies to the west of Santiago, on the coast. Pilgrims refer to it as the "End of the World," because this is as far west as the Camino will take you before spilling into the ocean. About four more days of walking.

Luc and I didn't say much as we packed our things in the morning. He walked me as far as the archway leading to the front of the cathedral, where I would find yellow arrows pointing away from the city and toward the coast. We embraced in the middle of the empty street for a long time, the sounds of clinking coffee mugs on tables at a café nearby. I have no idea what we said to each other. A fire in my heart seized me and I felt an overwhelming joy at having met this man. It was goodbye, but it was not sad.

We finally let go and I walked away. He stood in the street watching me head West, framed by the stone angel and saint laden cathedral. I looked back a couple of times, his hands in pockets pose eventually blending in with the gray sculptures.

Passing the cathedral and down into the misty unknown, I saw a figure approach: it was the nun in a sweatshirt and comfy

---

Tarta de Santiago
Serves 6-8

This traditional cake has been served in Santiago over many, many years and to many, many pilgrims. It is normally embossed with the traditional cross of the Camino or baked into a shell shape, both of which can be done at home with the right tools.

6 eggs, separated
1 cup sugar
2 cups almond flour
1 orange, zested
1 lemon, zested
½ tsp almond extract
About 2 TBL powdered sugar for topping

Preheat oven to 350. Grease and flour an 11" cake pan. Spring form is easiest, however a regular cake pan or muffin tin will do, although you might want to line with parchment first as it is a batter that likes to stick. Using an electric or stand mixer, beat the egg yolks and sugar together until smooth. Add zests, extract, and almond flour and mix to combine.
In a separate mixing bowl, beat eggs white until stiff peaks form. Fold into the almond mixture. Bake for 40 minutes or until firm. Allow to cool before removing from pan. Dust with powdered sugar before serving.

---

shoes. I told her I was sure this was the right thing, to keep walking. She nodded and hugged me; we prayed and cried a little, too. The Earth under my feet guided me up and out of the city, the spires of the cathedral visible behind me from the wooded trail.

I passed a lot of pilgrims, having no interest in talking to any of them. Sitting by a stream for a lunch of sardines and bread, I was joined by a young Basque woman. Together we admired the stone town and matching bridge that almost melted into the natural landscape. She began an endless rant about some Canadian man who'd rejected her and whom she was following (although she insisted she was not following) to Finisterre. I hardly spoke as she went on and on and on, feeling the water coursing through my veins, my eyes fixed on the yellow arrows ahead.

The afternoon wore on, a cool cloudy one, taking us through woods and past little streams. Many people passed going the other direction, as it was common to walk the loop from Finisterre, to Muxia, and back to Santiago. In fact, I'd heard of pilgrims who looped around and around, unable to leave the trail, stuck in some kind of limbo.

I ditched my tagalong at the first opportunity, snagging the last bed in the *albergue* and making myself an absolute feast in the tiny kitchen by way of celebration: chewy Galician bread, soft cheese, fried eggs with spinach, and a huge wedge of green melon only for me. I sat in the sunny courtyard and spoke to absolutely no one.

The following days were solitary, lonely, and long. Unlike my journey to Santiago, I did not make any friends, and instead spent much of my time in prayer and meditation. I admired the sea, swam in clear waters with no one around, and ate lots of bread. All I knew was that putting one foot in front of the other was the right thing to do, and as those steps rolled out behind me, Finisterre was clearly where I needed to go.

One foggy morning after spotting a bed bug had motivated me to step out into the near darkness of the morning, I stopped to admire a crumbling, moss eaten chapel in a cemetery with tile letters spelling out its name. It felt like a secret moment only for me, as if I was the only person alive in that moment.

By mid-morning I'd spotted the first glimpse of ocean since leaving Asturias weeks before. It was rejuvenating, glistening from up high in a deep bay. I spent the afternoon picking sea glass from a tiny deserted beach and ate a perfect meal of beans, steak, and salad at an *albergue* with some old German women who complained about the fruit having spots. I hitched a ride back to the *albergue* from some spear-fishermen that was hunting for octopus at sunset. I barely made it by curfew.

In the morning of the final stretch into Finisterre, certain of my path, I came to a way marker asking pilgrims to choose between either Finisterre or Muxia (another popular pilgrim destination along the coast). As I considered taking the way to Muxia, I laughed heartily at myself and at life. I'd been so sure just moments earlier of taking the route to Finisterre, but all it took was the suggestion of another way to stir my certainty. And how beautiful it was to be given these choices—to know that life was not just a two-lane highway with our birthplace at one end and a hamburger joint at the other.

We have a path—the brief moments in life when we actually travel on it are the most incredible, but along our journey we choose. We choose all the time. Which way to go, how we will travel, who we will share these choices with. What a beautiful, beautiful life.

This time, I hooked a left toward Finisterre, leaving Muxia for another day.

thirty-three

After spending a couple of days on a balcony facing the ocean in Finisterre, it was finally time to go to the end of the world. I'd spent the days walking for hours on the beach in the late morning and in the evening, collecting colorful shells and watching the waves. The water was clear and the weather was sunny, and I spoke to no one for days except the lady at the coffee shop and the clerk at the hostel. I would sit on that balcony waiting for the sun to rise, drinking more cups of instant coffee than I care to admit, waiting for the right time to walk those final kilometers.

Just past Finisterre stood a lighthouse and the last official way marker of the Camino: 0.0 kilometers. At last I joined a string of packless pilgrims heading up the winding road and found a place on the cliff to watch the sun go down on this last gasp of pilgrimage. Facing the hot sun and the stretching ocean, I laid out my treasures: a hat from a friend, a well-worn sock with no mate, a small loaf of bread, foraged mint, and a tiny bottle of champagne.

I sat there looking out over the ocean, with my back against the rock and my legs out in front, too hot to do much else besides stare at the sea. When at last the sun began to sink down, I ate some bread, cheese, and sausage. Then I placed pieces of each inside the hat on a flat rock near a thorny little flower bush. Opening my wine, I thought of this guy Jesus. "This is my blood," I soaked a bit of the bread in wine, "This is my body." I ate it and drank a swig, "given for you." I poured a little into the hat and drank the rest. In a small way I'd given my body over, too. I'd given it bit by bit to the months of worry that had whittled me down to bones, to the Camino with all those forward steps, to Luc, to the choice to take up the cross and walk to the end of the Earth. And now, as I accepted the body and blood of Christ, on the ledge and with nowhere else to go, I understood that I didn't need to destroy myself, to purify, exorcise, or transform. What I needed was a little food. Without knowing it, I had been brought closer to God than I had imagined possible.

An orange sunset raged over my little shrine and tears came hot and hard. I needed to forgive myself for what I'd done: a failed marriage, a false life, living for another's dream, sacrificing my own sense of love, well-being, and self-respect. For praying to the God of relationships, for failing to see that God was there with me all the time, loving me and guiding me. For wasting years trying to force my way through life, for playing the victim at the expense of others. I was ashamed at all the time I'd wasted, for holding myself back, for blaming everyone and everything but me. And yet, I was here. Without those missteps my butt would not be on this rock, with 900 kilometers and the adventure of a lifetime behind me. It had to be this way.

So there on that rockside, the ocean swirling with foam, the currents pulling away and then surging back again, I began the journey toward forgiving myself, as Jesus had already done. "This is my body, given for you."

I had to become willing to make amends to myself for not living a life of perfection, to allow myself mistakes and failures.

I sat there in my own sweat, nowhere to go, no possible way to go further. It was time to let her go. Let go of the woman who'd let me down, who'd beat me up, who'd failed at morphing into someone she's not. I cried for her, for my old life, for those dreams that would never be. I sat there for hours, in silence, looking out at the ocean with my shoes off. When the sun finally sank I sang to it, sang to my old life, the Hawaiian chant of gratitude.

> "'Uhola 'ia ka makaloa lā
> Pū'ai i ke aloha ā
> Kūka'i 'ia ka loa lā
> Pāwehi mai nā lehua.
> Mai ka ho'oku'i a ka hālāwai lā
> Mahalo e nā akaua,
> Mahalo e nā kūpuna lā 'eā
> Mahalo me ke aloha lā,
> Mahalo me ke aloha lā"

And I let her go, that woman that I was not, with that last sunset at the end of the world. I accepted that I, that life, would never be the same. Going back wasn't an option, and now I knew it never was. It was time to move forward into the unknown, more vast and deep than the ocean in front of me, this time without arrows to follow.

recipes

acknowledgments

It doesn't feel like I wrote this book at all. It feels more like simply recording the sights, sounds, and of course the colorful people around me as they went about touching my life in deep and beautiful ways. Grateful is a humble word for how it feels to collect the stories of all your interesting, magnificent lives.

For those mentioned in this book, and especially you, thank you. Thank you for allowing me to tell how you impacted my life and to express the way I see your light. For those that read the early drafts, chapter by chapter, thank you. Your opinions, advice, and encouragement meant more than you know.

For those that housed, fed, and befriended me along this journey, thank you. Many strangers, family members, and

friends helped, welcomed, and cared for me at very great lengths along the way. If only all your names could be listed here.

To the patrons of Yellow Arrow Coffee, the Summit County Pilgrims and the town of Breckenridge, CO, thank you for welcoming me into your community and embracing my vision. Although we have since parted, I consider my year among you one of the best.

Thank you especially to Rachael, Christian, and Nai'a for adopting me. Thank you to Lisa for inspiring me to write this. Thank you, Aaron, for having full confidence in me without reading one word. And thank you to Peanut, for opening my soul completely.

Made in the USA
Charleston, SC
13 June 2016